HOW TO EAT YOUR FEELINGS

working through emotions, one recipe at a time

Middleton Public Library
7425 Hubbard Avenue
Middleton, WI 53562

HOLLY HAINES

CONTENTS

01 Introduction

03 Annoyed

11 Anxious

21 Bored

31 Coldblooded

41 Confused

51 Happy

67 Lonely

79 Messy

89 Sad AF

101 Stressed

111 Thankful

Acknowledgements

Layout design and author photograph by Mikee Catacutan

Illustrations by Carolyn Ramos

Photography by Holly Haines

All of the recipes in this book are truly personal and influenced by all of the people that have blessed my life. You are all essential. Thank you to my mom Betty and sister Tina for their support in every project I pursue. I would also like to thank Jonathan Waecker, Chantal Pasag, JerVae Anthony and Mikee Catacutan for always having my back, my front, plus my sides, too. Also, shoutout to me for writing and photographing a whole book.

Introduction

I didn't realize how often I used cooking as a form of meditation until I began looking back through my recipes and thinking about what was happening at the time they were written. Then, I saw the pattern. I make bread when I'm stressed. I make dim sum when I'm anxious. I crave Filipino food when I'm a tainch lonely.

I use cooking to transform my feelings into something tangible, into something I can taste, and these are some of my favorite recipes I've cooked on my journey.

Let me give you one piece of advice for cooking these recipes, or any recipe for that matter:

When you're cooking, **cook**.

Be mindful. Use all of your senses. Feel the cool steel of the knife between your fingers. Smell the fresh herbs as you chop. Look over at the sauce, it's just beginning to bubble. Listen to the sizzle of a piece of bacon hitting a hot skillet. And, most importantly, taste everything along the way.

ANNOYED

Look. When I'm annoyed, I want to chop things very, very hard, but I don't necessarily feel like cooking a whole meal. These are dips and sauces that help me get out that energy, via mortar and pestle or aggressive herb chopping.

Toum (Lebanese garlic sauce) (pg. 04)

Corn salsa (pg. 07)

Baba ganoush (pg. 07)

Smoked almond gremolata (pg. 09)

Feeling kinda annoyed.

Toum

Southern Californians may know this as the cracky garlic sauce you get at Zankou Chicken. You can put this on anything to give it a punchy kick of garlic deliciousness. It's great with pita bread, on top of chicken or tossed in with a little sauteed shrimp and pasta.

MAKES 1/4 CUP IN ABOUT 10 MINUTES

10 cloves garlic, peeled

sea salt

1/2 cup vegetable or grapeseed oil

1/2 lemon, juiced

Mash the garlic: Add the garlic to a mortar with a generous pinch of sea salt. Mash until a smooth paste forms.

Add in the oil: Grind in the oil about 1 teaspoon at a time, making sure the oil has been fully absorbed and incorporated before adding more. Alternate adding lemon juice and oil. It'll take about 10 minutes to incorporate the oil. Taste and adjust lemon juice and salt as needed. The texture should be thick and viscous.

Feeling kinda annoyed.

Corn salsa

My friend Mikee calls this "corn crack". Crack, indeed. This is another super versatile condiment. Eat it with tortilla chips as a snack or add it to a quick bowl of chicken, rice and beans for some burrito bowl feels.

MAKES 3 CUPS ABOUT 10 MINUTES

Cook the corn: Wrap corn (with husk and silk still on) in a slightly damp paper towel and microwave on high for 4-5 minutes. Let cool, then remove silk and husk. Cut corn away from cob.

Roast the poblano: Using an open stove top flame or a broiler, char the poblanos all over. Place the charred peppers in a bowl and cover with plastic wrap for about 5 minutes. This helps steam the skin off. Let cool slightly, remove stems, seeds and most of the charred skin, and dice.

Mix it all together: In a medium bowl, stir together corn with chopped poblano, red onion, jalapeno, cilantro, lime juice and olive oil. Season with 1/2 tsp each of salt and pepper. Taste; adjust salt, pepper and lime juice as needed.

Notes: You can use a bag of thawed frozen corn in a pinch but it's so much better with fresh corn.

3-4 ears of fresh sweet corn (see notes)
2 large poblano peppers
1/2 red onion, diced
1 jalapeno, diced
1 bunch cilantro, stems removed and chopped
1 lime, juiced, more to taste
1 tbsp olive oil
salt and pepper

Baba ganoush

Lots of furious chopping in this recipe - perfect for when you're annoyed. There's also something cathartic about flaming an entire eggplant.

MAKES 1/2 CUP ABOUT 40 MINUTES

Cook the eggplant: Broil eggplant on a baking sheet or over an open flame on the stove top, turning every few minutes, until charred all over. Place in a large bowl and cover with plastic wrap and let cool, about 30 minutes. This helps to steam off the skin.

Combine it together: Remove the eggplant from the bowl, saving any liquid the eggplant released. Peel off most of the charred skin and chop (leave a few charred bits in for that smoky flavor). In a medium bowl, combine the eggplant, a couple spoonfuls of the eggplant liquid, parsley, olive oil, garlic, tahini, lemon juice and zest, and about 1/2 tsp of salt. Taste, and adjust lemon juice and salt as needed. Garnish with a drizzle of olive oil and fresh parsley.

2 large eggplant
1/4 cup parsley, chopped, plus more for garnish
3 tbsp olive oil, plus more for serving
2 garlic cloves, minced
2 tbsp tahini
1/2 lemon, zest and juice
kosher salt, to taste

Feeling kinda annoyed.

Smoked almond gremolata

I know I said I put the Toum (pg. 4) on everything but I also put this on everything. This is a nice little condiment to keep around in the fridge - it really just brightens everything up, like a little spoonful of sunshine. Put it on top of broiled fish and veggies for a quick and light dinner.

MAKES 1/2 CUP IN ABOUT 10 MINUTES

Make garlic paste: Using the side of a large knife, mash the garlic together with a good pinch of salt until it forms a paste. You can also do this in a mortar and pestle.

Mix it together: In a medium bowl, combine garlic paste, lemon juice and zest, red pepper flakes, olive oil and white wine vinegar. Stir in parsley and almonds. Taste; adjust salt, oil and vinegar as needed.

2 cloves garlic, peeled
kosher salt
1 lemon, zest and juice
1/4 tsp red pepper flakes
1/4 cup olive oil
2 tsp white wine vinegar
1/2 bunch chopped fresh parsley
1/4 cup smoked almonds, finely chopped

ANXIOUS

I need something tedious and time consuming. I need to keep my hands busy. I really need to zone out for a good amount of time but not really have to think too hard.

It's time for dumplings.

Mushroom and quinoa potstickers (pg. 13)

Pancit molo (pg. 14)

Lamb dumplings in chili sauce (pg. 17)

Lumpia (pg. 18)

Feeling kinda anxious.

Mushroom & Quinoa Potstickers

Ahhhh, a perfectly long and tedious activity to take your mind off of whatever is making you anxious. Making the pleats is key to how a potsticker cooks, so take your time; there is a purpose to the detailed madness. The pleats create a dumpling shape with a flat surface on the bottom that helps them sit up real pretty.

MAKES ~50 POTSTICKERS IN ABOUT 1 HOUR 15 MINUTES

---

for the potstickers

- 1 lb mushrooms, chopped
- 2 cups chopped baby bok choy
- 1 cup cooked quinoa, cooled
- 1 cup green onion, finely chopped
- 1 tbsp ginger, minced
- 1 tbsp sugar
- 1 tbsp sesame oil
- 1 tbsp soy sauce
- 1 tsp cornstarch
- 1 tsp ground pepper
- 1/2 tsp salt
- 1-2 cups chicken broth, vegetable broth or water
- 50-60 gyoza / potsticker wrappers
- vegetable oil
- hot mustard, for serving

for the dipping sauce

- 1/4 cup black vinegar
- 2 tbsp soy sauce
- 1 tbsp ginger, julienned

Cook the mushrooms: Add 1 tbsp of oil to a very hot pan. Add in chopped mushrooms and sauté until nicely browned and their liquid has evaporated, about 6-8 minutes. Turn off the heat and add in bok choy. Stir together, letting the residual heat from the pan wilt the bok choy. Let cool slightly, about 10 minutes.

Season the veggies: In a medium bowl, combine mushrooms and bok choy with quinoa, green onion and ginger. Add in the sugar, sesame oil, soy sauce, cornstarch, salt and pepper. Taste and adjust salt and pepper as needed.

Fold the potstickers: Place 1 heaping teaspoon of filling onto the middle of one wrapper. Dip your finger in some water and wet the entire perimeter of the wrapper. Fold in half like a taco, without sealing, then starting at one end, begin to pinch the seam together, followed by a pleat along one side of the wrapper (doesn't matter which side you pleat, as long as you're only pleating one side consistently) and another pinch. Continue to pinch and pleat along the edge of the potsticker – about 5-6 pleats per dumpling.

Cook the potstickers: Heat about 1 tbsp of vegetable oil over medium-high heat in a nonstick skillet that has a lid. Place potstickers in the pan seam-side up, being careful not to overcrowd the pan and making sure that they don't touch. Once the bottoms have browned nicely, about 4-5 minutes, add in about 1/4 cup of chicken broth and quickly place the lid on the pan. Be careful, the oil will splatter once you add in the broth. Let the potstickers steam and absorb the broth – about 5 minutes. Repeat in batches with remaining potstickers. Serve with dipping sauce and hot mustard

Make the dipping sauce: Combine all ingredients in a small bowl. Adjust soy sauce and vinegar to taste.

Note: These freeze great! Place potstickers on a parchment-lined baking sheet, making sure they aren't touching. Freeze until frozen solid, about 3-4 hours. Store in an air-tight container.

Feeling kinda anxious.
Pancit molo

If your Filipino grandma made wonton soup, I think it would sort of come out like this. I love folding these little dumplings, the finished product looks like a little wonton giving itself a hug.

MAKES 4 SERVINGS IN ABOUT 1 HOUR 30 MINUTES

---

for the broth

1 quart organic chicken stock

2 bay leaves

1 medium onion, diced

3 cloves garlic, peeled

1 tsp salt

1 tsp whole black peppercorns

1 lb chicken, bone in (legs or thighs)

water

1 tbsp fish sauce (Patis), or more to taste

for the dumplings

1 lb ground pork

1/2 lb shrimp, peeled, deveined and minced

1/2 cup green onion, finely chopped

1 tsp sesame oil

1/2 cup onion, finely chopped

2 cloves garlic, minced

1 egg

1/4 tsp salt, more to taste

freshly ground pepper, to taste

~60 wonton wrappers

for serving

chopped green onions

fried garlic

Make the broth: In a large stock pot, place chicken stock, bay leaves, diced onion, garlic, salt and whole peppercorns and bring to a boil. Add in chicken pieces and additional water (enough to cover the chicken, about 4 cups) and simmer over medium-low for 2 hours. Skim off any impurities that come to the surface. The broth should be rich in flavor, but not salty – the salt will come from the addition of fish sauce (patis) later.

Remove the chicken from the stock. Once cool enough to handle, discard the skin and bones and shred chicken meat. Set aside.

Make the filling: In a medium bowl, combine the ground pork, minced shrimp, green onion, sesame oil, white onion, garlic, egg, salt and pepper. Take the time to fry up a small patty of the mixture to check for seasoning – you can't season once the filling is inside the wrapper. Adjust seasonings as needed.

Fold the dumplings: Place 1/2 tbsp of filling in the center of the wrapper. Wet the perimeter of the wrapper with your finger. Join opposite corners of the wrapper together to form a triangle. Carefully seal the edges together, making sure you're pushing out any air bubbles around the filling. With the top of the triangle pointed away from you, fold the left and right sides over each other, using a little water to seal the edges. It should look like the dumpling is giving itself a nice, tight hug. Repeat.

Cook the dumplings: In a medium or large pot, place shredded chicken and add 1 tbsp of fish sauce (patis) and saute over medium high heat for a couple of minutes. Add 7-8 cups of stock to the pot and bring to a boil. Add in dumplings, no more than about 15 at a time, and cook about 6-8 minutes. They'll float to the top once they're done. Cook in batches as needed. Garnish with green onions and fried garlic, or serve with white rice.

Feeling kinda anxious.

Lamb dumplings in chili sauce

This recipe was born of my obsession with Din Tai Fung's chili dumplings. This is my version, with a lamb twist. Feel free to substitute the lamb for chicken or pork.

MAKES 50 DUMPLINGS IN ABOUT 1 HOUR 15 MINUTES

---

for the chili sauce

- 3 tbsp soy sauce
- 2 tbsp chili in oil, more to taste
- 2 tbsp Chinese black vinegar
- 1 tbsp tahini
- 1/2 tsp sugar
- 1 garlic clove, minced
- 1 green onion, diced
- 1/4 cup crushed roasted peanuts

for the wontons

- 1 pound ground lamb
- 3 tbsp Shaoxing wine
- 3 tbsp soy sauce
- 3 tbsp ginger, grated
- 3 tbsp green onions, finely minced
- 1/2 tsp salt
- 1 tsp ground white pepper
- 1/4 tsp Sichuan peppercorns, ground; more to taste
- 1 package (50-60) fresh wonton wrappers

Make the sauce: Combine all sauce ingredients, minus the crushed peanuts and stir thoroughly. Set aside while you make the wontons.

Make the filling: In a medium bowl, combine the ground lamb, 3 tbsp Shaoxing wine, 3 tbsp soy sauce, ginger and green onions, Mix thoroughly. Season with salt, white pepper and Sichuan peppercorns and continue to mix until the mixture resembles a paste. Take the time to fry up a small patty of the mixture to check for seasoning. You can't season once the filling is inside the wrapper, so do yourself a favor and try it out before you start filling the dumplings. Adjust seasonings as needed.

Fold the dumplings: Place about 1/2 tbsp of filling in the center of a wonton wrapper. Using a bit of water, wet the perimeter of the wrapper with your finger. Join opposite corners of the wrapper together to form a triangle. Carefully seal the edges together, making sure you're pushing out any air bubbles around the filling. With the top of the triangle pointed away from you, fold the left and right sides over each other, using a little water to seal the edges. It should look like the dumpling is giving itself a nice, tight hug. Repeat.

Cook the dumplings: Bring a large pot of water to a boil. Stir the water and gently drop the dumplings in, being careful not to crowd them. Stir occasionally to make sure they don't stick. Adjust the heat to keep the water at a simmer, and cook for 3-5 minutes or until the wrappers begin to look translucent and the dumplings float.

Drain cooked dumplings and place in a serving dish. Top with sauce and garnish with crushed peanuts and additional green onion, if desired.

Feeling kinda anxious.

Lumpia

Lumpia is probably the most recognizable Filipino food. If you've ever been to a Filipino party, you know there's always a huge metal tray of these babies waiting to be devoured. Once you get into the groove of rolling these up, the process goes swiftly.

MAKES 50-60 IN ABOUT 1 HOUR 30 MINUTES

- 3 tbsp water
- 3 tbsp soy sauce
- 3 tbsp cornstarch
- salt and pepper
- vegetable oil, more for frying
- 3 cloves garlic, minced
- 1/2 tsp chili flakes, more to taste
- 1 lb ground pork
- 1 lb ground beef
- 3 green onions, chopped
- 1/2 cup shredded carrots
- 3 cups shredded cabbage
- 50-60 lumpia or eggroll wrappers, separated
- sweet chili sauce, for dipping

Mix the sauce: Combine water, soy sauce, cornstarch, 1/4 tsp each salt and pepper.

Cook the filling: Heat 1 tbsp oil in a large pot. Add garlic and chili flakes and sauté until fragrant, about 30 seconds. Add ground beef and pork, cook thoroughly. Drain most of the fat from the pan. Add in green onion, shredded carrots and cabbage; cook for 2 minutes or until cabbage begins soften. Reduce heat to medium-low.

Add the sauce: Stir the soy cornstarch mixture (the cornstarch might have settled) and add to the pot. Stir well. This should bind all of the ingredients together without being too saucy. Taste, and adjust soy sauce and chili flakes as needed. Let mixture cool to room temperature.

Roll the lumpia: Lay one wrapper down with a corner pointed toward you. Place about 1 tbsp of filling near the corner of wrapper closest to you, about the size and shape of your pinky finger. Fold the corner closest to you up over the filling, rolling the mixture up tightly; after the first full roll, fold in the sides of the wrapper toward the center, making sure to keep the wrapper pretty tight around the filling, but not tight enough to break the wrapper. Wet the tip of the end of corner with a bit of water and seal.

Fry the lumpia: Heat about 2" of oil over medium-high heat to about 350F. Cook until wrapper is browned and crispy all over. Drain on paper towels. Serve with chili sauce.

BORED

I need a project. I need something detailed and involved with a sweet payoff. I want that sense of accomplishment you only get when you do something super science-y in the kitchen and it actually comes out delicious. I want to spend too much time waiting for things to rise and watching liquids reduce. I want my Instagram Stories to be a million annoying slits across your feed but you keep coming back 'cause you wanna know what I end up making. I'm bored, man.

Marsala mushroom lasagna (pg. 23)

Pretzel bread pudding with brown sugar bourbon (pg. 24)

Brown butter caramel rice krispie treats (pg. 27)

Honey pandesal (pg. 28)

Feeling kinda bored.

Marsala mushroom lasagna

Sometimes I just want to eat a bunch of mushrooms, and what better vehicle for mushroom mouth delivery than lasagna? Making a bechamel isn't nearly as intimidating as it seems, just pay attention to it. Using no-boil noodles makes the rest of this recipe a breeze.

MAKES 6-8 SERVINGS IN ABOUT 1 HOUR 20 MINUTES

for the mushrooms

- 3 tbsp butter
- 1 medium onion, finely chopped; divided
- 3 cloves garlic, chopped
- 2 lbs crimini mushrooms, sliced
- 1 1/2 cups marsala wine
- 1 tsp chopped fresh thyme

for the bechamel

- 6 tbsp butter
- 5 tbsp flour
- 5 cups milk
- 1/4 tsp freshly grated nutmeg

for the lasagna

- 1 box (~9 oz) no-boil lasagna noodles
- 2 cups shredded mozzarella cheese
- 1 cup Parmesan cheese

Cook the mushrooms: Heat butter in a large skillet over medium-high heat. Reserve 2 tbsp of chopped onions for the bechemel, and add remaining to the pan along with garlic; saute for 2-3 minutes. Add in mushrooms and turn heat to high. Cook until tender, stirring often. about 10 minutes. Add in thyme and marsala wine. Cook until most of the liquid evaporates, about 15 minutes. Add salt and pepper to taste. Remove from heat.

Make the bechamel: Add 6 tbsp butter to a heavy saucepan over medium heat. Add in 2 tbsp reserved onion and cook until softened. Stir in flour and cook for about 3 minutes, stirring the entire time. Whisk in the milk and bring to a simmer, stirring constantly, until it begins to thicken. Be sure to scrape the bottom and edges of the saucepan. Cook until the mixture is thick enough to coat the back of a spoon. You should be able to draw a clean line with your finger through the sauce on the spoon without the sauce running. Add nutmeg and salt and pepper to taste. Stir in the mushrooms and remove from the heat.

Put the lasagna together: Heat the oven to 350F. Butter a 9x13" casserole dish and place a thin layer of the bechamel and mushrooms on the bottom. Top with a layer of noodles, 1/3 each of the bechamel and mushrooms, Parmesan and mozzarella cheese. Repeat layers again, ending with the mushroom bechamel layer topped with mozzarella and Parmesan. Cover with foil and bake for 30 minutes. Remove the foil and bake an additional 10-15 minutes, until the top is lightly browned. Let cool 10 minutes before serving.

Feeling kinda bored.
Pretzel bread pudding

This recipe can be adjusted to just how bored you really are. If you're SUPER bored, make the pretzel rolls from scratch (see page 107). If you're not quite that bored, use store-bought pretzel rolls.

MAKES 6-8 SERVINGS IN ABOUT 2 HOURS

for the bread pudding

- 8 pretzel rolls, torn into 1-inch pieces (about 8-9 cups)
- 2 cups heavy cream
- 2 cups whole milk
- 5 green cardamom pods, cracked
- 4 eggs, beaten
- 1 1/2 cups sugar
- 1 1/2 tsp vanilla extract

for the sauce

- 1/2 cup unsalted butter
- 1 cup brown sugar
- 2 tbsp heavy cream
- 4 tbsp bourbon
- 1 pinch flaky sea salt

Toast the bread: If you're using super fresh bread, you can lightly toast the bread pieces for 15 minutes in a 350F oven. It'll dry the bread out a bit and allow for more of the custard to be absorbed. If you're using day-old / stale bread, you can skip this step.

Infuse the milk: In a small saucepan, combine 2 cups heavy cream and 1 cup of milk over medium heat. Add cracked cardamom pods. Stir to combine, and heat mixture until it becomes steamy and barely starts to bubble. Remove from heat, cover, and let the spices steep in the milk for 30 minutes. After steeping, strain mixture into a large bowl. Set aside and let cool until lukewarm.

Make the custard: Preheat oven to 350F and lightly butter a 9x13 inch casserole dish. In the large bowl combine the cream, remaining 1 cup of milk, eggs, sugar and vanilla. Whisk to combine. Pour the mixture over the torn pretzel bread. Set aside for 20 minutes, allowing the bread soak up the custard mixture. Press down the bread pieces every few minutes to ensure all pieces are absorbing the custard.

Bake the pudding: Bake at 350F for 45-60 minutes. A toothpick inserted should come out clean and dry. If it's still a bit jiggly after 45 minutes, bake longer, checking every 5 minutes. The pudding should be slightly puffed and browned.

Make the sauce: While the bread pudding is baking, combine butter, sugar, heavy cream and bourbon in a heavy saucepan over medium heat. Stir constantly, mixture comes to a boil and sugar has dissolved. Remove from heat and stir in sea salt. Store any leftover sauce in the refrigerator.

Serve bread pudding warm or room temperature.

25

Feeling kinda bored.
Brown butter caramel rice krispie treats

Have you ever had a homemade rice krispie treat? It's really the bee's knees. It's also the bee's upper body and stinger when you add homemade salted caramel to the mix.

MAKES 8 TREATS IN ABOUT 1 HOUR

for the caramel
- 1/2 cup granulated sugar
- 4 tablespoons unsalted butter, room temperature
- 1/4 teaspoon flaky sea salt
- 3 tablespoons heavy cream, room temperature

for the treats
- 1 stick (8 tbsp) unsalted butter, plus extra for the pan
- 1 10-ounce bag marshmallows
- 1/4 teaspoon coarse sea salt
- 6 cups Rice Krispies cereal

Make the caramel: Set a square of parchment paper over a medium-sized plate. Lightly butter or spray the parchment with non-stick spray.

In a medium, dry saucepan over medium heat, melt the sugar; this will take about 5 minutes. Do not stir the sugar (really, don't), but swirl the pan around to dissolve any pockets of unmelted sugar. By the time it is all melted, if should be a nice amber color; if not, cook until it is. This happens quickly, and you can go from caramel to burnt sugar quickly, so keep an eye on it. Remove the saucepan from heat and stir in butter; it may not incorporate entirely. Stir in cream and salt and return saucepan to the stove over medium-low heat, bringing it back to a simmer and melt any sugar that solidified. Cook the caramel a few minutes more, until slightly darker.

Pour out onto parchment-covered plate and transfer plate to the freezer for 10-15 minutes, until soft and pliable and no longer liquid. Form caramel into large marble-sized pieces.

Brown the butter: Butter an 8x8x2" pan. In a large pot, melt 1 stick butter over medium-low heat; resist the urge to do this over high heat, you'll just burn the butter and have to start over. The butter will melt, then foam, then turn clear golden and finally start to turn brown and smell nutty. Stir frequently, scraping up any bits from the bottom as you do.

Make the treats: As soon as the butter smells nutty and takes on an amber color, turn the heat off and stir in the marshmallows. The residual heat from the melted butter should be enough to melt them, but if it isn't, turn the heat to low until the marshmallows are smooth. Add in the salt. Remove the pot from the stove and add in cereal. Once most of the marshmallow is incorporated, stir in chunks of caramel. Try not to over mix, and work quickly – you want to be able to see swirls of caramel throughout. Quickly spread into prepared pan using a silicone spatula or a piece of wax paper to press down. Let set for about 30 minutes.

Feeling kinda bored.

Honey pandesal

Pandesal is a traditional Filipino bread roll, usually enjoyed with some type of margarine or coconut jam or butter and a cup of sweet and creamy coffee. My version is a bit on the sweeter side, using honey instead of sugar in the dough.

MAKES ~24 ROLLS IN ABOUT 2 1/2 HOURS

- 1 1/4 cup whole milk, warmed to ~100F
- 1 packet (2 1/4 tsp) active dry yeast
- 1/2 cup honey, divided
- 2 cups all-purpose flour
- 2 cups bread flour
- 1 tsp baking powder
- 1 tsp salt
- 1 large egg, beaten
- 1 tbsp vegetable oil
- 6 tbsp butter, melted
- 1 cup bread crumbs

Proof the yeast: In a medium bowl, stir together warm milk, yeast and 1/4 cup of honey. Let the yeast proof for about 10 minutes; you'll know the yeast is working when you see bubbles forming at the surface.

Make the dough: In a large bowl, combine both all-purpose and bread flour, baking powder and salt. Whisk the dry ingredients together, then stir in the milk-yeast mixture, remaining 1/4 cup of honey, beaten egg, vegetable oil and melted butter. Once a dough starts to form, turn out onto a lightly floured surface. It'll be slightly sticky; flour your hands as needed. Knead the dough until smooth and elastic, about 10 minutes. Add about 1/2 tbsp of oil into a clean bowl. Place the dough in the bowl, turning over in the oil so the dough is coated. Cover with a clean tea towel and let rise in a warm place until doubled, about an hour.

Form the rolls: Pre-heat oven to 375F. Punch down the dough and turn out onto a clean surface. Divide into 4 equal pieces. Place the dough you're not working with back into the bowl and cover with the towel so it doesn't dry out. Gently roll the dough into a cylinder about 6" long and cut, on the diagonal, into 6 equal pieces. Dip each slice in bread crumbs and place on a parchment or Silpat-lined baking sheet, bread crumb side up. Repeat with remaining dough. Cover with a clean tea towel and let rise another 30 minutes.

Bake the rolls: Bake for 20-25 minutes, until just golden and the house smells delicious. Eat warm, with butter or cheese or honey or coconut jam or nothing at all. Store leftovers in an airtight container.

COLDBLOODED

I'm lowkey wondering why other people even exist at all? If this mood were a major arcana tarot card, she'd be The Hermit reversed. Sort of anti-people and extra sensitive to strangers, but not really sure why. I need something smokey or spicy or stew-y to warm up my cold heart.

The recipes in this chapter use a stovetop smoker, which you can find online at Amazon.com. You can also do a DIY version: Line a roasting pan with foil and add in woodchips. Top with a chips with a drip tray fashioned out of a couple layers of foil. Add a roasting rack on top of the foil drip tray, and place your food on the rack. Cover the entire pan tightly with more foil and smoke away.

Or just buy a stovetop smoker, it's like $35. And if you have a real smoker, I'm jealous.

Chipotle turkey chili (pg. 33)

White beans with smoked turkey (pg. 34)

Smoked honey wings (pg.37)

Smoked chicken and dumplings (pg. 38)

Feeling kinda coldblooded.

Chipotle turkey chili

The chipotle gives this chili such a comforting and warm smoky flavor. Feel free to double up on the chipotle and make her a bit more spicy.

MAKES 4 SERVINGS IN ABOUT 1 HOUR

---

1 tsp dried sage

1 tsp cumin

1 tsp dried rosemary

1 tsp dried thyme

1 tsp dried oregano

1 tsp salt

1 tsp pepper

2 whole chipotle peppers in adobo sauce, chopped

4 strips bacon, chopped

1 onion, diced

3 cloves garlic, chopped

2 lb ground turkey

2 cans white beans, drained

2 cups chicken broth

cilantro, green onions, sour cream for serving

Make the spice mix: In a small bowl, stir together sage, cumin, rosemary, thyme, oregano, salt and pepper and chipotle peppers.

Cook the meats: Heat a dutch oven over medium-high heat. Add in chopped bacon and cook until crispy. Remove bacon (leave the bacon fat in the pot) and set aside. Add onions and garlic to the bacon fat. Cook until onions are translucent. Add in chipotle spice mix and cook another minute or so. Add in ground turkey and cook until no longer pink.

Let it simmer: Add in beans and chicken broth. Simmer for 30 minutes, stirring occasionally.

Garnish with bacon. Serve with chopped cilantro, green onions, and sour cream.

Feeling kinda coldblooded.

White beans with smoked turkey

Listen. I love a big ol' bowl of creamy, smoky beans over a pile of hot white rice. It's the stuff coldblooded comfort food is made of. Using a pressure cooker not only cuts down on the cooking time, but you can also skip soaking the beans beforehand.

MAKES 6 SERVINGS IN ABOUT 1 HOUR AND 30 MINUTES

- 2 tbsp olive oil
- 1 large onion, diced
- 3 stalks celery, sliced
- salt and pepper
- 1 tbsp creole seasoning (like Tony Chachere), more to taste
- 3 cloves garlic, chopped
- 3 sprigs fresh thyme
- 2 bay leaves
- 4 links chicken sausage, sliced
- 1 lb dried white beans
- 1 smoked turkey leg
- 6 cups chicken stock
- ~6 cups cooked white rice, to serve
- chopped green onion, for garnish

Sweat the vegetables: In a pressure cooker over medium heat (at least 6 quarts), add in olive oil. Once hot, add in onion and celery. Cook over medium heat for about 8 minutes; vegetables should be soft and cooked through. Season with about 1/4 tsp each salt and pepper and 1 tbsp creole seasoning, garlic, thyme, bay leaves and sausage. Increase the heat to medium-high and cook until the sausage has browned a bit, a few minutes.

Cook the beans: Add the beans and the turkey leg to the pot, followed by the chicken stock. Be sure to follow your pressure cooker's manufacturer's instructions for limits on the amount of liquid that can be added to your pressure cooker. The beans should be completely covered by chicken stock, but take care not to go over your pressure cooker's "max fill line".

Bring the cooker up to full pressure. Once pressure has been reached, reduce the heat just enough to maintain pressure, then start timing for one hour. After one hour, turn off the heat and allow the pressure to come down naturally.

Taste and season: Remove the lid and taste - adjust the seasonings and, if necessary, cook a bit longer (sometimes a few of the beans are little under cooked and need another 15 minutes or so of cooking - uncovered with no pressure).

Remove the turkey leg from the pot and let cool enough to handle. Shred the meat, discard the bone, and add the smoked turkey back to the beans.

Serve with hot white steamed rice and garnish with green onion.

35

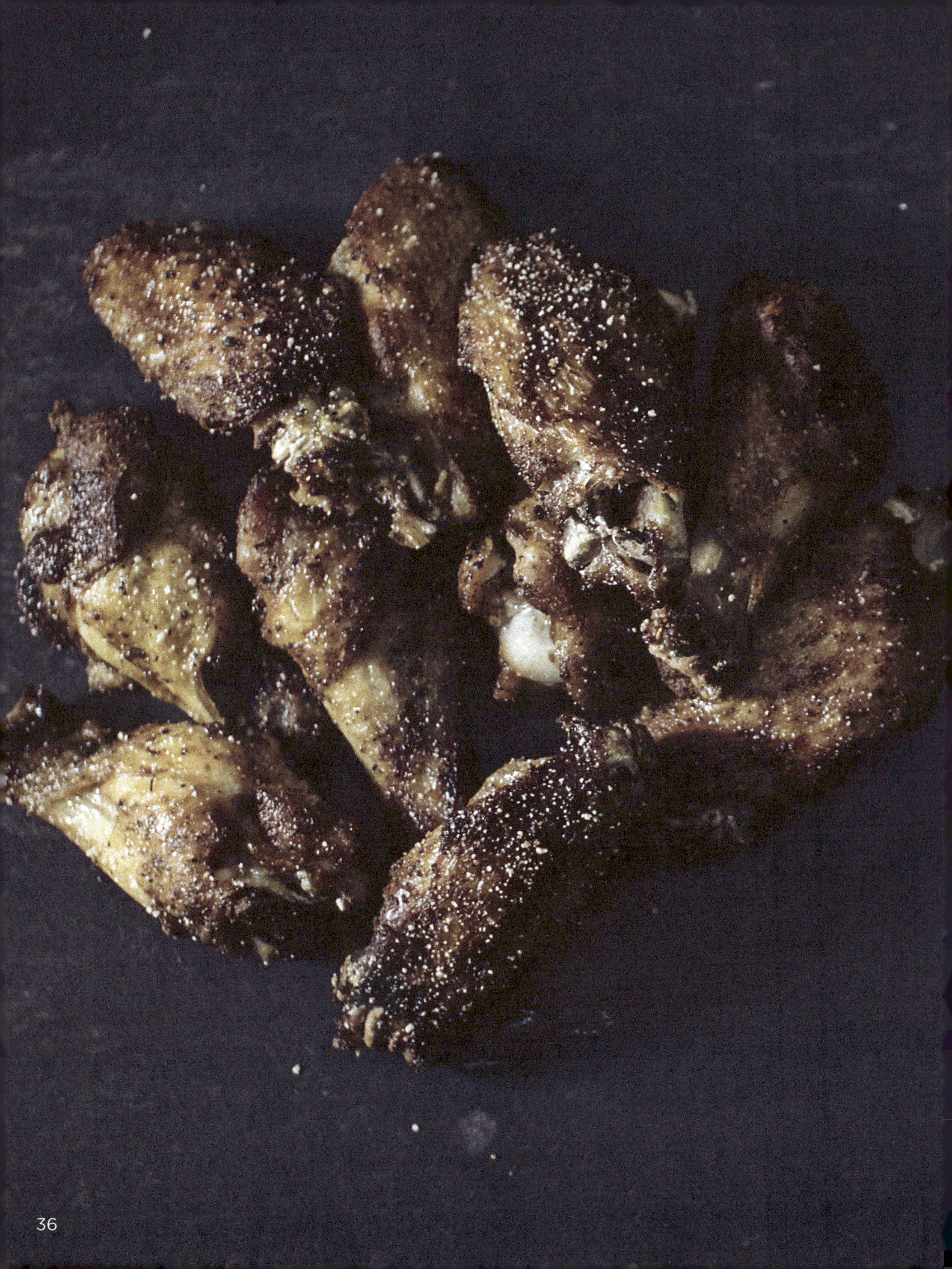

Feeling kinda coldblooded.
Smoked honey wings

This is the recipe that made me fall in love with my stove top smoker. Smoked chicken wings are a revelation.

MAKES 4 SERVINGS IN ABOUT 1 HOUR 30 MINUTES, PLUS TIME FOR RESTING

---

1 cup whiskey

1/2 cup brown sugar

1/2 cup coarse sea salt

2 tbsp whole black peppercorns

6 garlic cloves, crushed

2 lemons, 1/4" slices

30-40 wings, split at the joint

2 tbsp apple wood chips (or your favorite fruit wood)

2 tbsp creole seasoning

2 tbsp dehydrated honey powder (see notes)

peanut or vegetable oil, for frying

Brine the wings: Combine whiskey, brown sugar an sea salt in a large container large enough to contain all of the chicken and 8 cups of water. Alternately, you can split the ingredients evenly between two large gallon re-sealable bags (which is what I prefer). Add in 1 cup of hot water to dissolve the sea salt and brown sugar. Once dissolved, add in peppercorns, crushed garlic, lemon slices and chicken wings. Add 8 cups of cold water. Refrigerate and let brine for at least one hour, and up to 6. Any longer than 6 hours and your wings may get too salty from the brine.

Rinse chicken and discard brine. Pat chicken dry with paper towels.

Smoke the wings: Place wood chips at the bottom of your smoker pan, followed by the drip tray. Place wings on a rack inside the drip tray and fit with lid. Smoke over medium-low heat for 1 hour. Let rest and cool completely, at least one hour, or keep refrigerated up to 3 days.

Fry the wings: In a medium bowl, combine 2 tbsp creole seasoning and 2 tbsp honey powder and set aside. Heat about 3" of oil in a large pot or a deep fryer to 450F. Fry until skin is golden and crispy, about 6-8 minutes. Drain wings on paper towels and immediately season with spicy honey powder mixture.

Notes: You can find dehydrated honey powder at Asian markets or on Amazon.com.

Feeling kinda coldblooded.

Smoked chicken and dumplings

It tastes like a bowl of Thanksgiving.

MAKES 4 SERVINGS IN ABOUT 1 HOUR

---

for the soup

3 lbs chicken thighs, boneless and skinless

2 tbsp hickory wood chips

salt & pepper

2 tbsp butter onion, diced

4 ribs of celery, sliced thin

2 tbsp all-purpose flour

4 cups of chicken stock

2 bay leaves

1/2 tsp dried basil

1/2 tsp dried thyme

for the dumplings

1 1/2 cups all-purpose flour

2 tsp baking powder

1/2 tsp salt

3 tbsp cold butter, cubed

3 tbsp chopped parsley

3/4 cup milk, more as needed

Smoke the chicken: Season chicken with salt and pepper. Using a stove top smoker, smoke chicken over oak wood for 20 minutes. Let cool and shred into bite-size pieces.

Start the soup: While the chicken is smoking, start on the soup. In a large pot, melt butter and saute onion and celery over medium heat for a few minutes. Sprinkle in the flour and cook for 2 minutes to cook out the raw flour taste. Slowly pour in chicken stock, being careful to whisk continuously as you do to prevent lumps. Add in bay leaves, 1/2 tsp black pepper, basil and thyme. Simmer for about 15 minutes. Add in the chopped chicken and continue to simmer. While simmering, start on the dumpling dough.

Make the dumplings: In a large bowl, combine 1 1/2 cups of flour, baking powder and salt. Whisk to combine. Work the cubed butter into the flour with a pastry cutter (or your finger tips) until the mixture resembles coarse crumbs and the butter is broken down into tiny pea-sized pieces. Add in chopped parsley. Add in milk. This mixture is moist, but not super wet. Just use enough milk to bring the mixture together. If you need more, add in 1 tbsp at a time until the mixture comes together.

Cook the dumplings: Make sure your broth is at a gentle simmer, but not boiling. Drop in rounded tablespoonfuls into the simmering stock, trying to keep dumplings from touching each other. Cook, uncovered, for about 10 minutes to let the dumplings set. Cover and simmer an additional 8-10 minutes until dumplings are cooked through and tender.

Garnish with some additional chopped parsley.

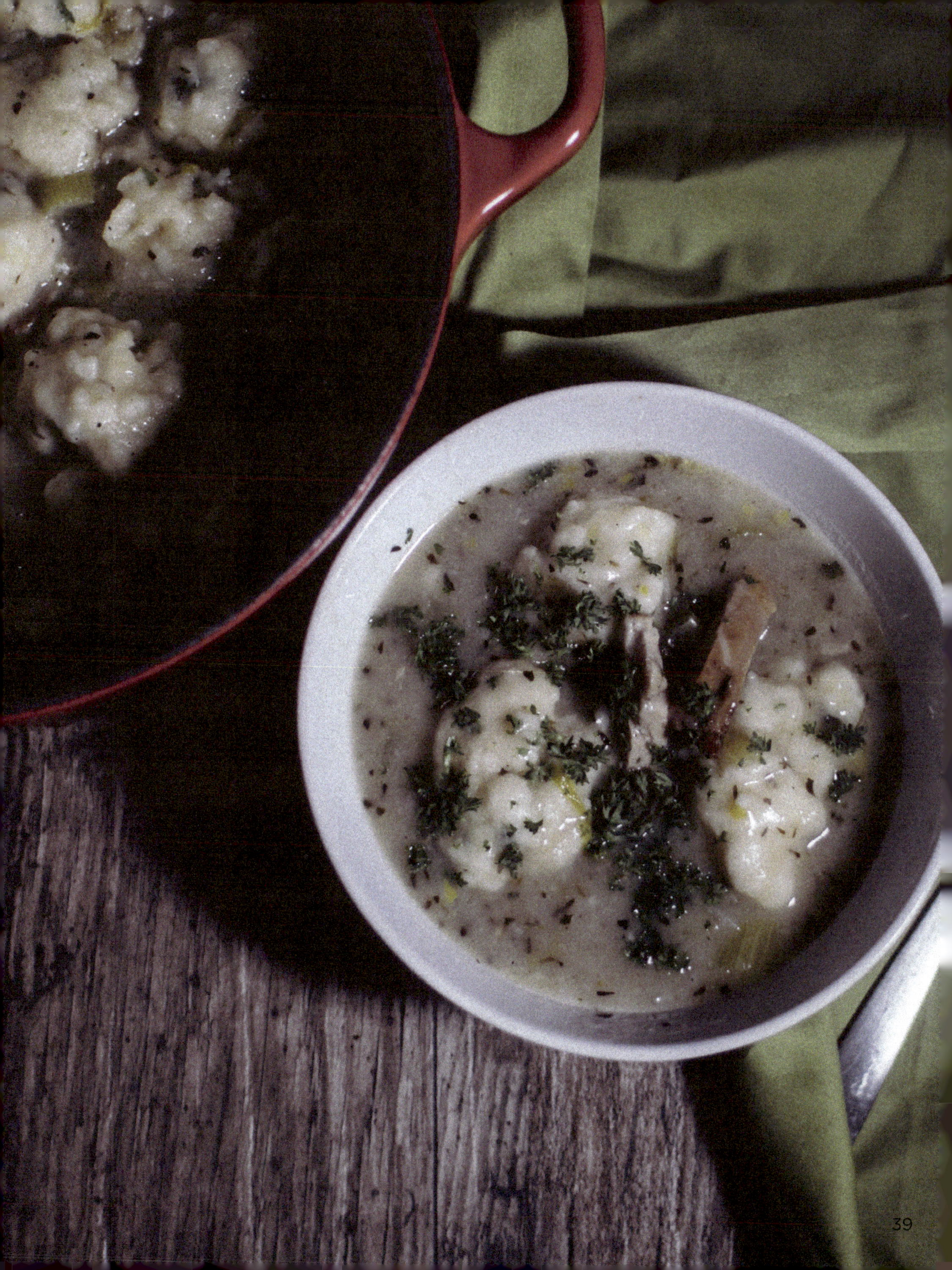

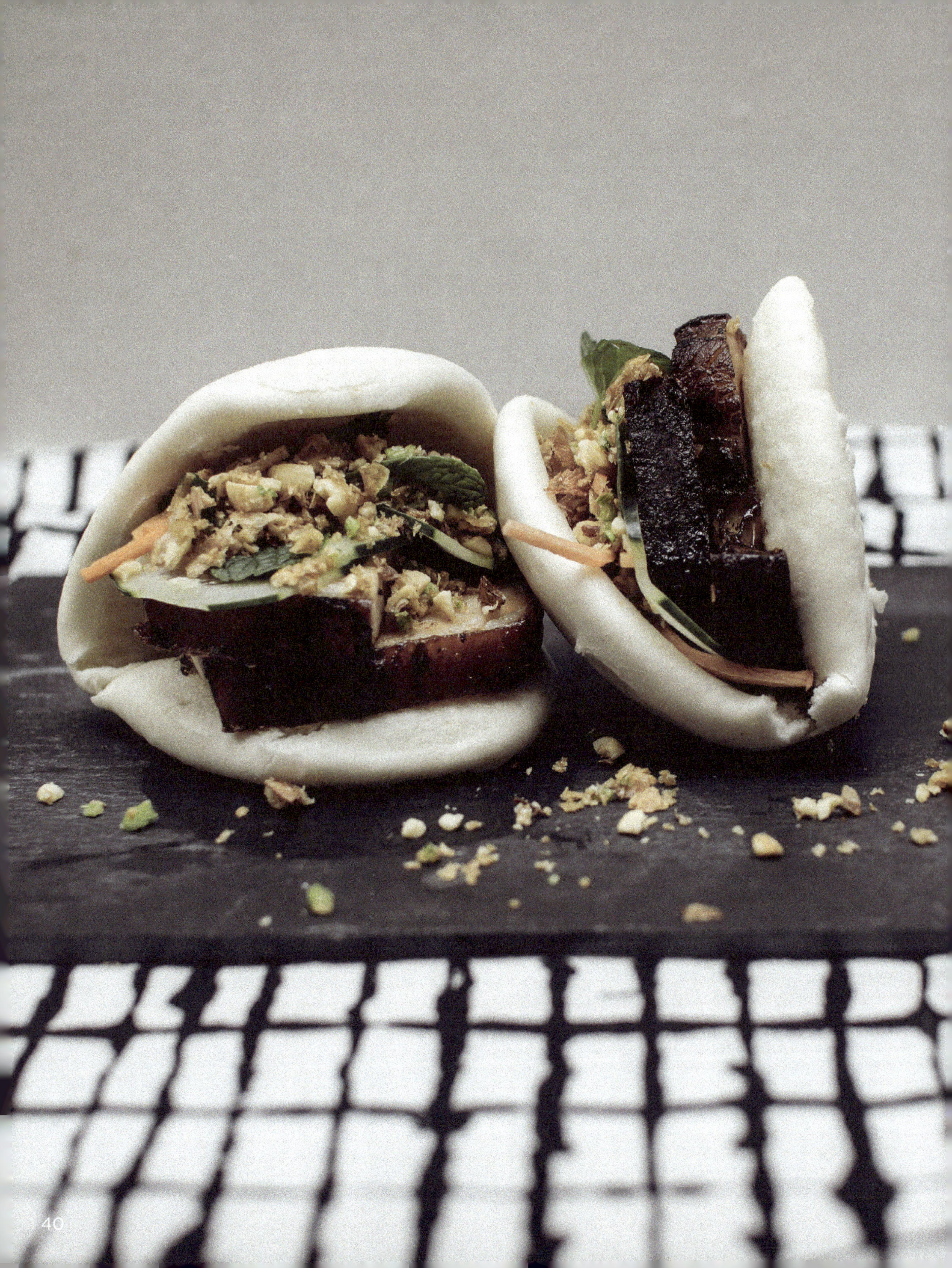

CONFUSED

Why are you like this? Why am *I* like this? I don't know what I want, but I definitely know what I don't want.

These recipes are a mash-up of different cravings because sometimes that's what life does... it shows us a bunch of things we don't want so we get a better idea of what we do want. And, I find that most times, the end result is unexpectedly delightful.

Jerk pork belly bao (pg. 43)

Po mì (pg. 44)

Korean BBQ tostadas (pg. 47)

Vietnamese fried chicken bun (pg. 48)

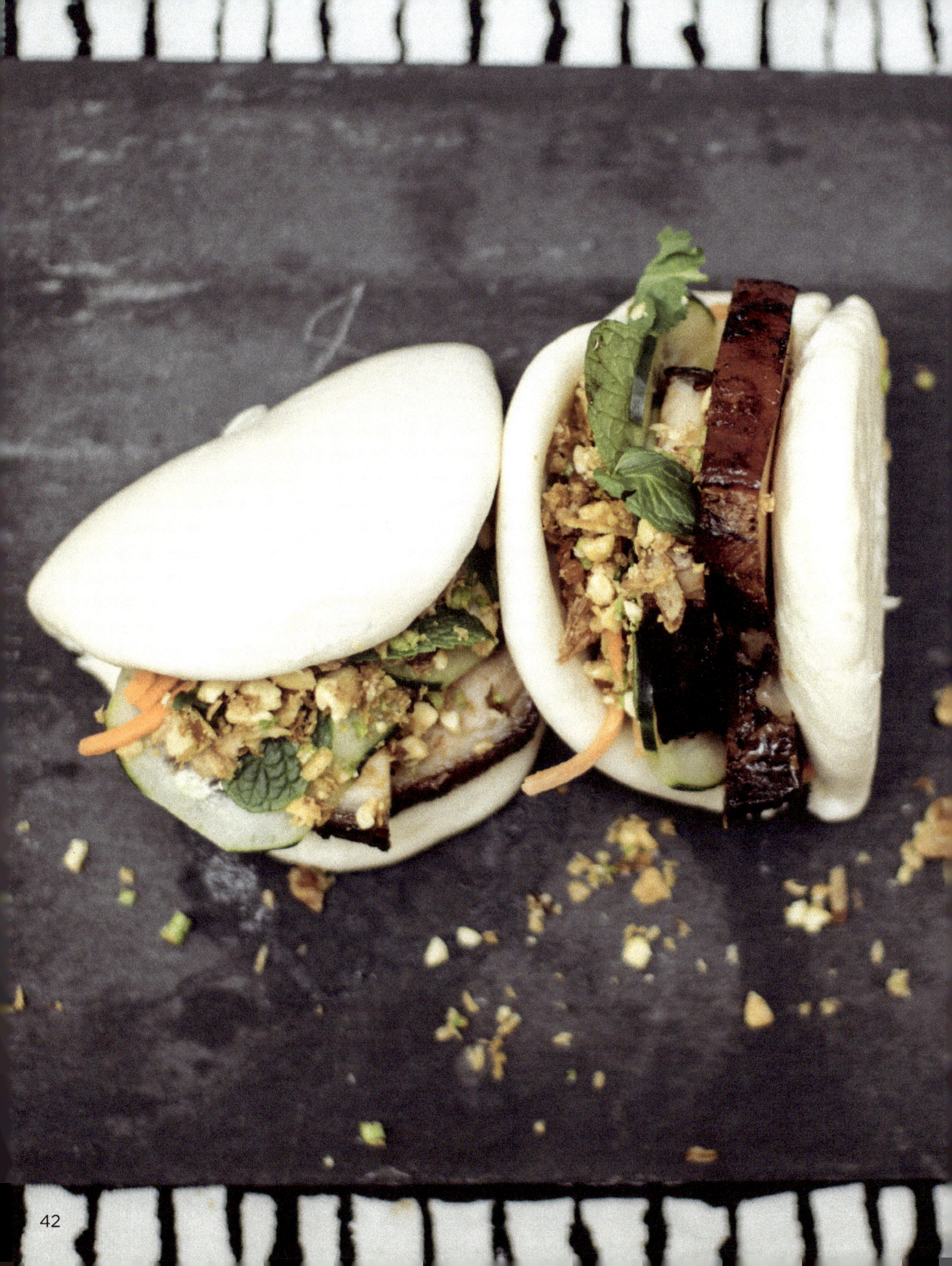

Feeling kinda confused.
Jerk pork belly bao

I really really wanted to make a Jamaican-style jerk pork belly, but I wasn't sure what to do with it. Then boom, BAO.

MAKES ~24 BAO IN ABOUT 4 HOURS, PLUS TIME FOR MARINATING AND CHILLING

---

for the pork belly

2 lbs pork belly

1/4 cup Walkerswood Jerk Seasoning

2 tbsp soy sauce

1 bunch green onions, chopped

1 onion, chopped

2 tbsp malt vinegar

3 sprigs fresh thyme

2 sprigs fresh rosemary

for the glaze

1/4 cup rice vinegar

1/2 cup brown sugar

1 tsp grated ginger

1 tsp grated garlic

1/4 tsp ground allspice

2 sprigs thyme

2 tbsp chopped green onions

1 tbsp Walkerswood Jerk Seasoning

for the bao

24 store-bought steamed buns

1/2 cup shredded carrots

1/2 cup sliced cucumbers

1/2 cup chopped green onions

1/4 cup chopped peanuts

1/2 cilantro leaves

1/4 cup fried shallots

Marinate the pork belly: Combine pork belly with jerk seasoning, soy sauce, green onions, onion, vinegar, thyme and rosemary. Marinate at least 4 hours, up to overnight.

Roast the pork belly: Preheat oven to 300F. Wrap pork, skin side up, in a double layer of foil and seal tightly. Cook on a baking sheet for 2 1/2 hours, until tender. Open up the foil packet so that the skin is exposed. Turn heat up to 450F and roast until skin is golden and beginning to crisp up in spots, about 20 minutes. Let cool to room temperature then chill for 3-4 hours or overnight.

Cut into pork belly into 1/4" strips and cook in a skillet over medium-high heat until warmed through.

Make the glaze: Combine all glaze ingredients in a small saucepan over medium-low heat until sugar dissolves and mixture thickens slightly, about 8 minutes. Set aside.

Make the bao: Steam the buns according to package instructions (usually 20 minutes in a steamer, or 20 seconds in the microwave). Add a few slices of pork to each bun, then top with glaze, vegetables and herbs as desired.

Notes: Please don't substitute the Walkerswood. It's essential. I've seen it in major grocery stores and on Amazon.com.

Feeling kinda confused.

Po mì

All the deliciousness of crunchy fried shrimp you'd find in a po boy with the brightness of pickled vegetables and herbs you'd usually find in a bánh mì. It's a Po mì.

MAKES 4 SANDWICHES IN ABOUT 1 HOUR 20 MINUTES

for the pickled veggies

- 1 cup carrots, cut into matchsticks
- 1 cup daikon radish, cut into matchsticks
- 1 tsp salt
- 1/2 cup plus 2 tsp sugar
- 1 cup distilled white vinegar
- 1 cup warm water

for the shrimp

- vegetable oil, for frying
- 1/2 cup cornmeal
- 1/2 cup flour
- 2 tbsp creole seasoning (like Tony Chachare)
- 2 eggs, beaten
- 1 lb large shrimp, peeled and deveined

for the sandwich

- 4 French rolls or 8 slider buns, or your favorite bread
- mayonnaise
- cilantro
- jalapeños, thinly sliced
- Maggi seasoning
- hot sauce

Quick-pickle the veggies: Place the carrot and radish in a bowl and sprinkle with 1 tsp salt and 2 teaspoons of the sugar. Use your hands to knead the vegetables for about 3 minutes. This helps remove some of the liquid from the veggies. Once they soften, liquid will pool at the bottom of the bowl. Stop kneading when you can bend a piece of carrot so that the ends touch but doesn't break. Drain in a colander and rinse under cold running water, then press gently to remove extra water. Transfer to a clean jar.

Combine the remaining 1/2 cup sugar, vinegar, and the water and stir to dissolve the sugar. Pour over the vegetables. The brine should cover the vegetables; add more vinegar if needed. Let the vegetables pickle for at least 1 hour before eating. They will keep in the refrigerator for up to 4 weeks.

Fry the shrimp: In a large skillet, heat about 1/2" of vegetable oil over medium-high heat. Combine the cornmeal, flour and creole seasoning in a bowl and mix well. Dip the shrimp in beaten eggs, then dredge in the cornmeal mixture. Fry until cooked through and crispy, about 2-3 minutes.

Make the sandwich: Split your bread in half and spread both sides with a thin layer of mayonnaise (or more to taste). Sprinkle with hot sauce and Maggi seasoning. Place shrimp down, followed by cilantro, pickled veggies, and thinly sliced jalapeno. Devour.

45

46

Feeling kinda confused.
Korean BBQ tostadas

I wanted kalbi ribs. I wanted tostadas. So, here we are. I know this looks like a ton of ingredients, but really it's like the same 5 things over and over again.

MAKES 8 SERVINGS IN ABOUT 1 HOUR 20 MINUTES, PLUS TIME FOR MARINATING

for the short ribs
- 1/2 cup soy sauce (Kikkoman)
- 1/2 cup mirin (rice wine)
- 1/2 cup brown sugar
- 10 cloves garlic
- 2" ginger, peeled and sliced
- 1 small onion, roughly chopped
- 1 small Asian pear, peeled, cored and roughly chopped
- 1 tbsp sesame oil
- 1/4 cup gochujang
- 3 lbs Korean-style beef short ribs

for the refried beans
- 1 tsp sesame oil
- 1 clove garlic, chopped
- 1 can (12 oz) refried beans
- 1 tbsp gochujang

for the slaw
- 2 tbsp gochujang
- 1 tbsp sugar
- 1 tbsp mirin
- 1 tbsp sesame oil
- 2-3 tbsp warm water
- 2 cups shredded cabbage

for the sour cream
- 1/2 cup sour cream
- 1 tsp gochujang
- 1/2 lime, juiced
- salt & pepper

for assembly
- 1/2 cup crumbled cotija cheese
- 8 tostadas

Make the short ribs: Combine soy sauce, mirin, brown sugar, garlic, ginger, onion, pear, sesame oil and gochujang in a blender or food processor and puree. Marinate ribs in mixture for at least 4 hours, preferably overnight. Grill or broil for about 5-8 minutes per side, until desired doneness. Use kitchen shears to remove the meat from the bones; cut into strips.

Make the refried beans: Heat sesame oil over medium heat in a medium saucepan. Saute garlic for about 30 seconds, then add in refried beans and gochujang. Heat until warmed through.

Make the slaw: In a small bowl, stir together gochujang, sugar, mirin and sesame oil. Stir in 2-3 tbsp of warm water, to desired consistency. Dress the shredded cabbage with the gochujang dressing.

Make the sour cream: In a small bowl, combine sour cream, gochujang and lime juice. Season with salt and pepper to taste.

Make the tostada: Top one tostada with a couple spoonfuls of the refried beans. Top with meat from short ribs and spicy slaw. Drizzle spicy sour cream over the top and sprinkle with cotija.

Feeling kinda confused.
Vietnamese fried chicken bun

I love Vietnamese bun bowls as a quick, easy and not-so-heavy meal. But sometimes, I want fried chicken with that.

MAKES 4 SERVINGS IN ABOUT 1 HOUR 15 MINUTES

for the chicken

1 1/2 lbs chicken tenders
1" ginger, finely chopped
2 cloves garlic, chopped
2 tbsp soy sauce
1 tbsp fish sauce
2 tsp sugar
1/2 cup potato starch (see notes)
oil for frying

for the sauce

1/4 cup brown sugar
1/4 cup rice vinegar
1/4 cup fish sauce
1/4 cup water
2 limes, juiced
2 cloves garlic, minced
1" ginger, peeled and minced
1 red chili or jalapeno, chopped

for the bun

12 oz vermicelli rice noodles
2 green onions, chopped
1 carrot, shredded
1 cucumber, julienned into 3" strips
1 cup cilantro leaves, torn
1 cup mint leaves, torn
1 cup basil leaves, torn
1/4 cup crushed roasted peanuts
1/4 cup fried shallots

Make the chicken: Combine chicken, ginger, garlic, soy sauce, fish sauce and sugar; marinate for one hour. Heat 1" of oil in a large skillet. It's hot enough when you sprinkle in a bit of flour and it begins to sizzle. Toss a few tenders into the potato starch to coat evenly. Fry until chicken is cooked through, 5-7 minutes, and drain chicken on paper towels. Continue to cook chicken in batches. For extra crispy chicken, let cool and fry a second time until a deeper golden color is reached.

Make the noodles: Bring a large pot of water to a boil and add in vermicelli noodles. Stir; turn off the heat and let the noodles soften in the hot water, about 5-8 minutes. Drain and rinse with cold water. Set aside.

Make the bowls: Divide the noodles between 4 bowls. Top with carrots, cucumber and fried chicken. Add herbs, peanuts and shallots. Serve with sauce.

Notes: If you can't find potato starch, use a combination of half all-purpose flour and half cornstarch.

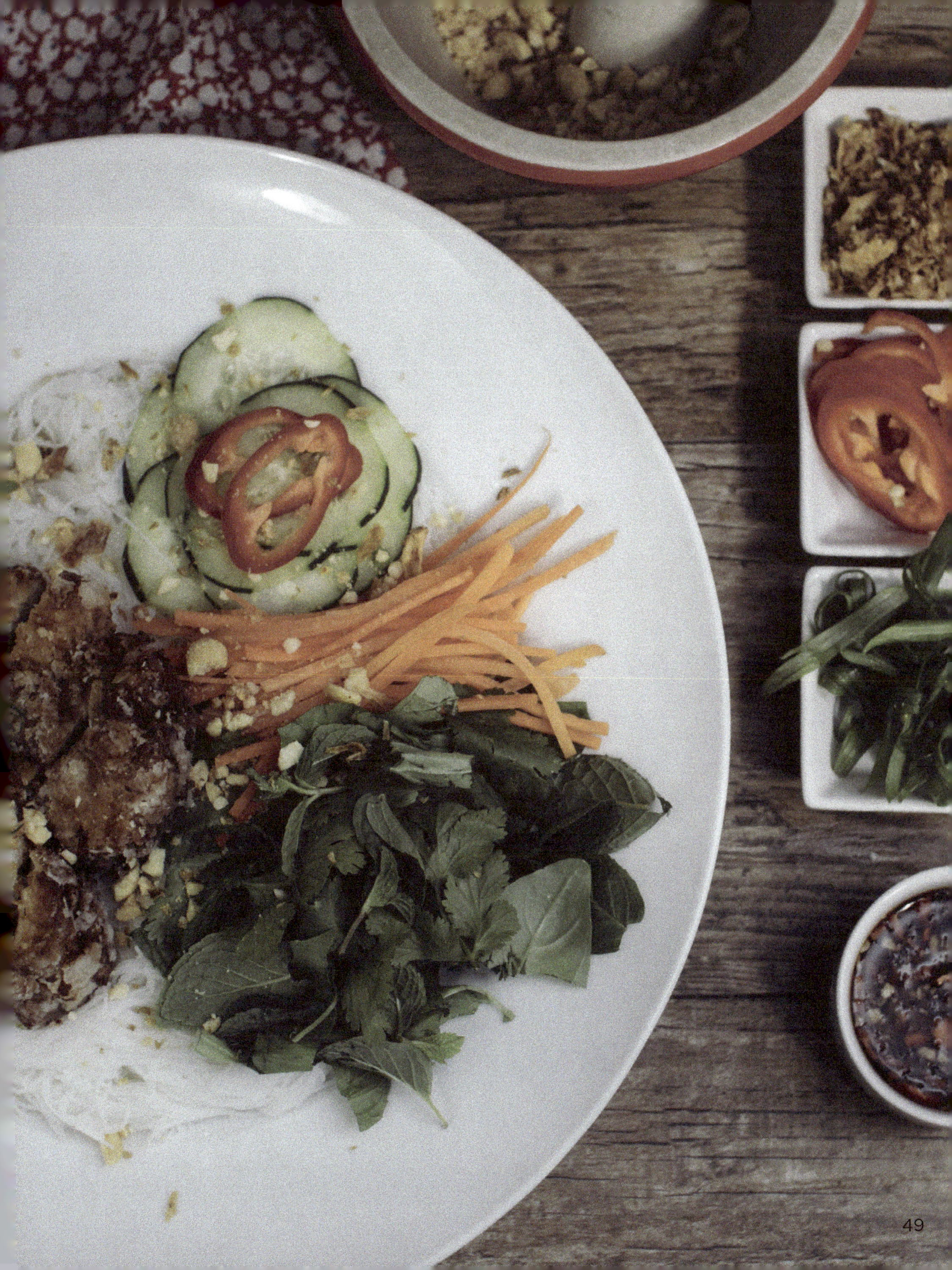

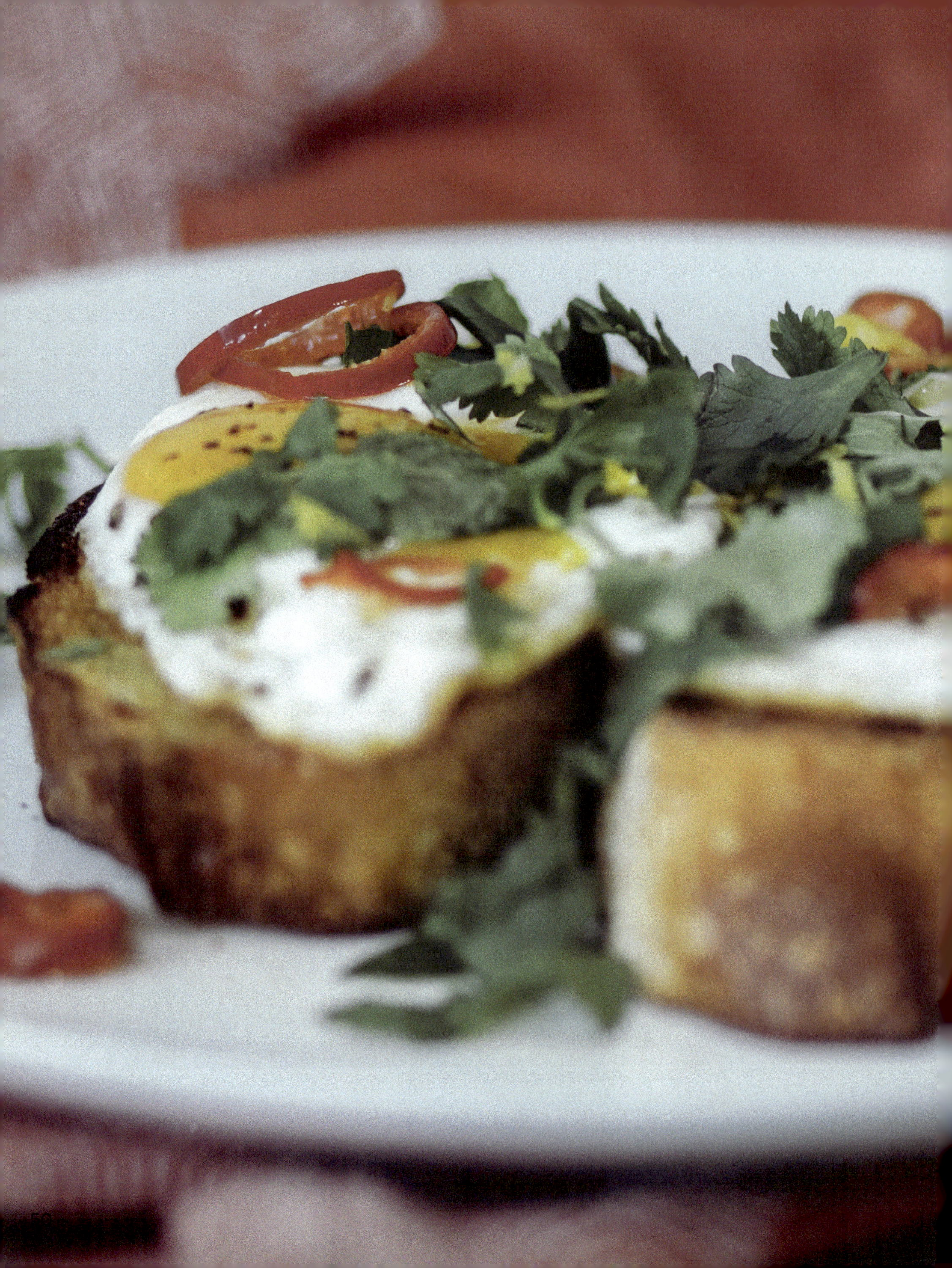

HAPPY

I'm feeling good. My body's feeling nice. My guts are acting right. My hair is growing and that little bald patch in my left eyebrow that I over-plucked 8 months ago finally came back. I've been meditating and taking my vitamins and probiotics. This is usually about the time a man comes into my life and fucks things up, BUT NOT THIS TIME SATAN.

I'd say I'm happy a strong 93% of the time, so these are my everyday, go-to recipes. I make all of these at least once a month. Highkey, this is my favorite chapter.

Brown butter chili eggs (pg. 53)

A good tuna salad (pg. 54)

Chicken shawarma with tabbouleh (pg. 57)

Peanut and lime sugar snaps (pg. 58)

Roasted brussels sprouts with garlic tahini (pg. 61)

Salmon with gremolata and baby broccoli (pg. 62)

$20,000 chocolate cake (pg. 65)

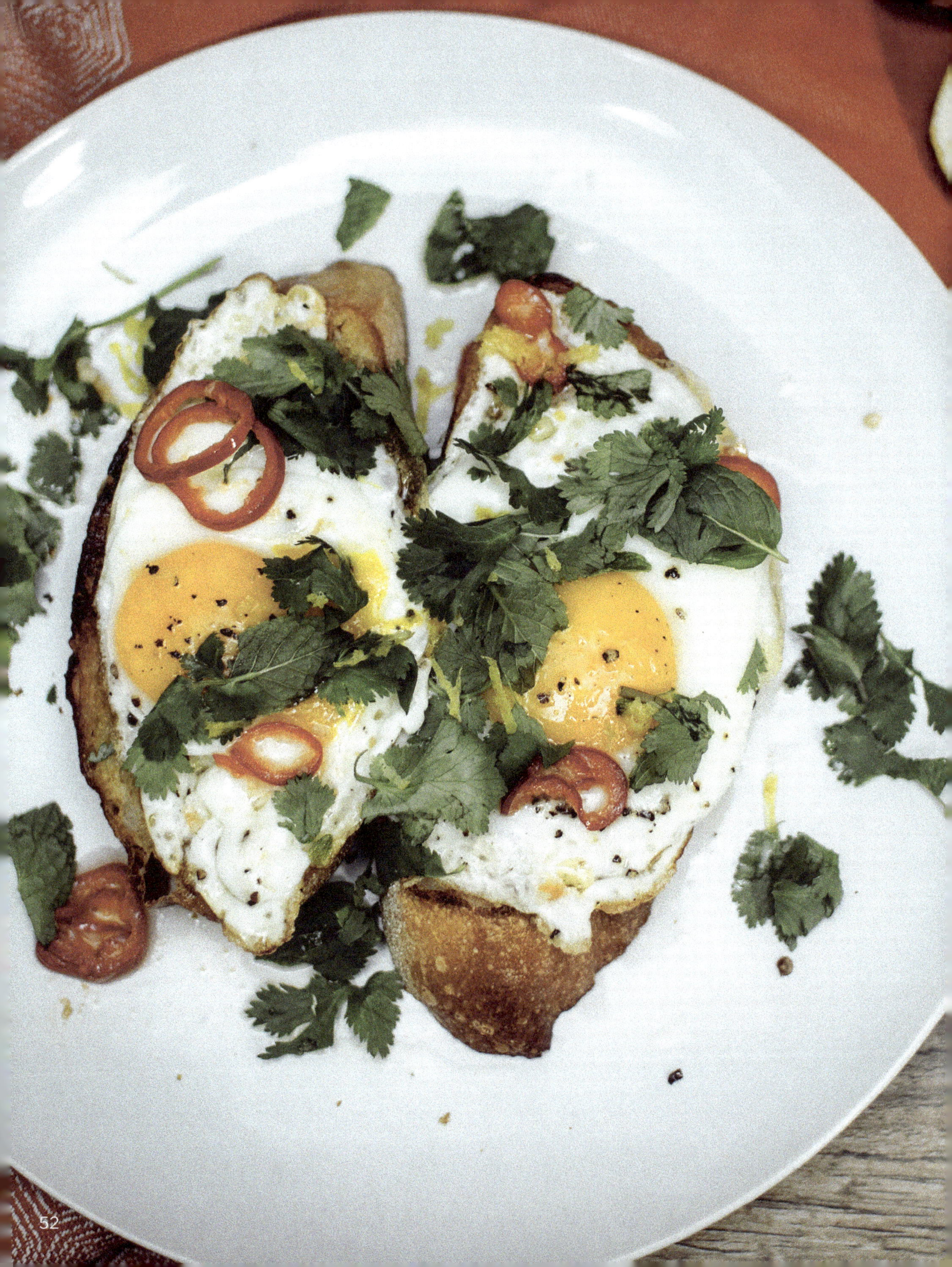

Feeling kinda happy.

Brown butter chili eggs

Brown butter makes everything better, really. These aren't your average over easy eggs - they're full of spice and bright flavors.

MAKES 2 BIG SERVINGS OR 4 LIGHT ONES IN ABOUT 45 MINUTES

- 4 slices of sourdough or french levain bread, about 1" thick
- olive oil
- 1/4 cup butter
- 2 cloves garlic, divided
- 1 red fresno chile, seeded and sliced
- 1/2 lemon, juice and zest
- 4 eggs
- salt and pepper
- 1/4 cup mint leaves, torn
- 1/4 cup cilantro leaves, torn

Toast the bread: Heat heavy skillet over high heat. Brush bread slices with a little olive oil on both sides and toast in the pan, a couple minutes per side. Cut one garlic clove in half and rub on one side of the toasts. Place the toast on a baking tray and keep them warm in the oven.

Brown the butter: In a small saucepan, heat butter over medium heat until a little brown and nutty-smelly, about 4-5 minutes. Stir in garlic, chilies and lemon juice; keep the butter warm in the oven with the toast while you fry the eggs.

Fry the eggs: In the same pan you toasted the bread in, turn heat to medium add about 1 tbsp olive oil into the pan. Crack in eggs and cook until yolk is at desired doneness.

To serve, place toast on plate and top with eggs. Drizzle brown butter over eggs and top with cilantro, mint, lemon zest and additional chilies if desired.

Feeling kinda happy.

A good tuna salad

I love a good tuna salad. This one is olive oil-based instead of mayo. It's great on toasty ciabatta as a sammich, a nice snack with crackers, fantastic on a bed of mixed greens and also great on a spoon, directly into your mouthmeats. Mix in whatever fresh herbs you have on hand. Basil, dill, cilantro, parsley... make this recipe yours.

MAKES 4 SERVINGS IN ABOUT 15 MINUTES

---

1 garlic clove, peeled

kosher salt and pepper

5 tbsp extra virgin olive oil

1/2 lemon, juice and zest

20 oz tuna, packed in olive oil, drained

2 tbsp capers, chopped

2 tbsp chopped green onion

2 tbsp chopped black olives

1/4 cup minced shallots

2 pepperoncinis, stems removed and chopped

4 ciabatta rolls

Make the dressing: Using a mortar and pestle (or a bowl and the back of a spoon), mash the garlic clove with a good pinch of kosher salt until it forms a paste. Add in olive oil, lemon juice and zest and stir to combine.

Put it all together: Combine tuna with the dressing, capers, green onion, olives, shallots and pepperoncini. Taste, and adjust olive oil, salt, pepper and lemon juice to taste. Serve on toasted ciabatta rolls.

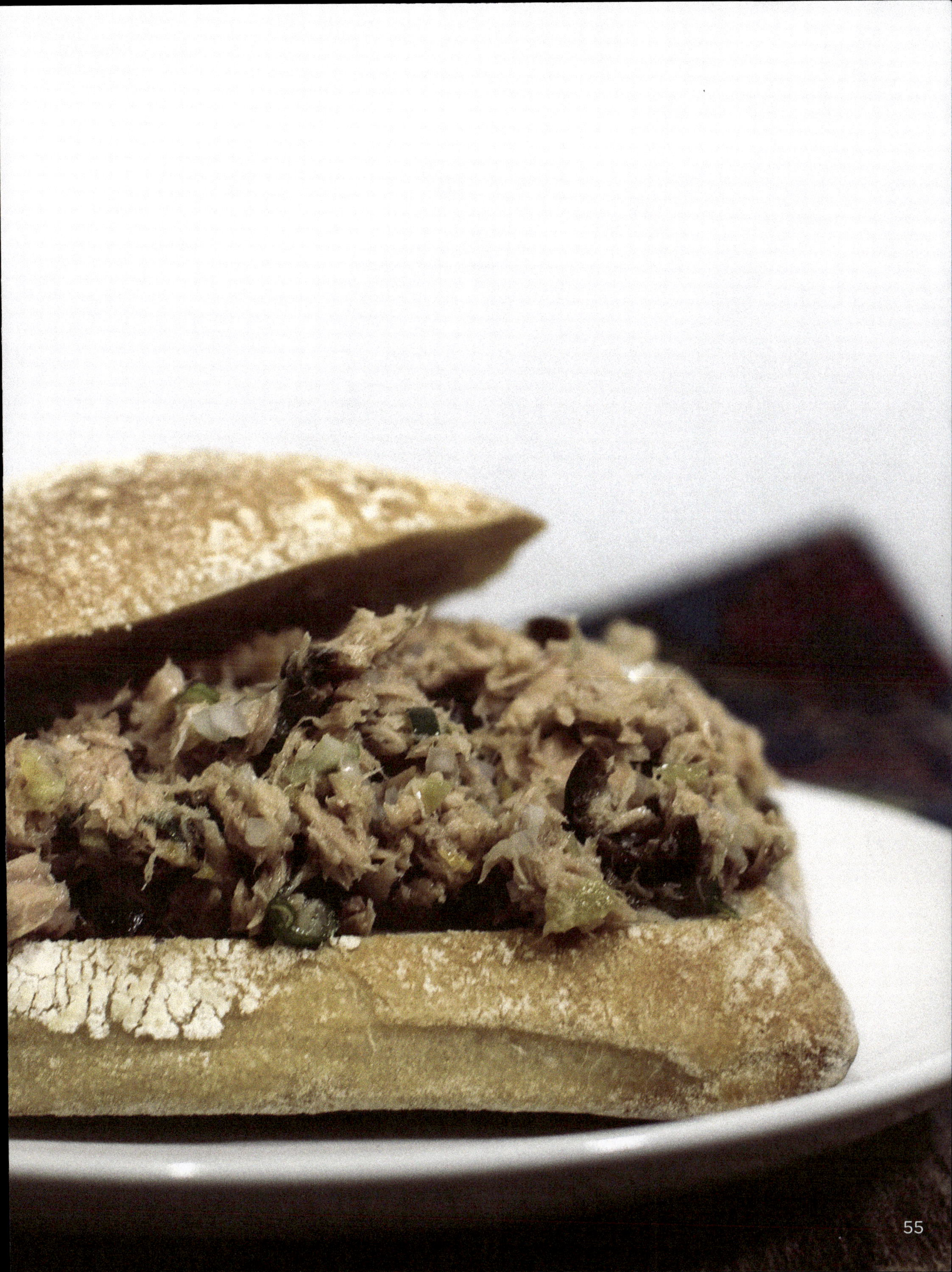

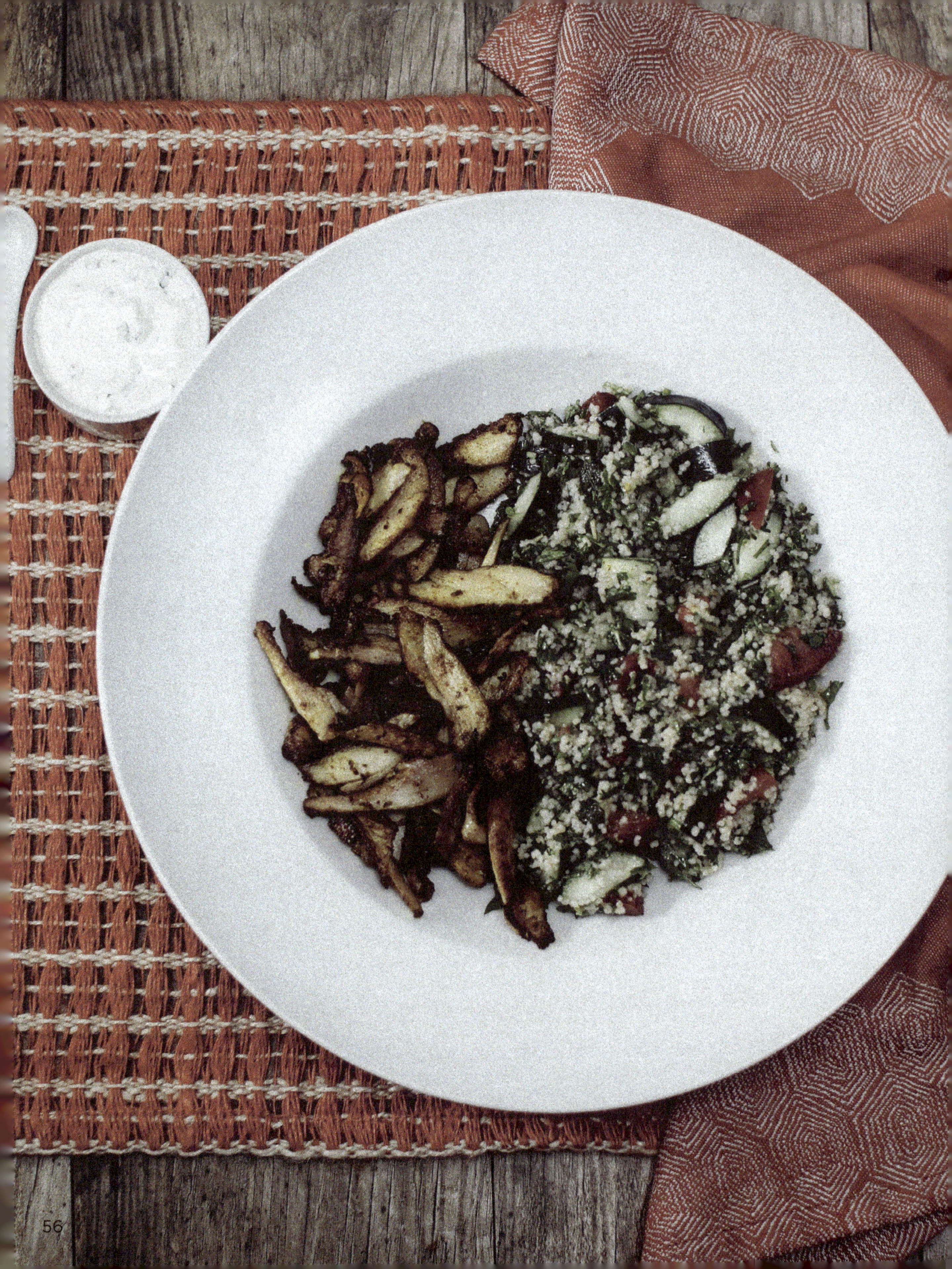

Feeling kinda happy.
Chicken shawarma with tabbouleh

This is one of my favorite quick meals. While the chicken is in the oven, you can make the tabbouleh and the sauce for a cute, quick little meal. This is also great for meal prepping!

MAKES 4 SERVINGS IN ABOUT 30 MINUTES

for the chicken
- 2 tsp cumin
- 2 tsp paprika
- 1 tsp allspice
- 1 tsp turmeric
- 1 tsp dried oregano
- 1/2 tsp garlic powder
- 1/2 tsp cinnamon
- 1/4 tsp chili flake (optional)
- Pinch of cayenne
- kosher salt and ground pepper
- 2 lbs boneless, skinless chicken thighs
- 6 tbsp extra virgin olive oil, divided

for the tabbouleh
- 1/2 cup fine couscous
- 1 lemon, juiced
- 3 tablespoons olive oil
- 1 cup boiling-hot water
- 2 cups finely chopped fresh parsley
- 1/2 cup finely chopped fresh mint
- 3 small tomatoes, cut into 1/4-inch pieces
- 1 seedless cucumber, peeled and cut into 1/4-inch pieces

for the yogurt sauce
- 1 cup greek yogurt
- 3 tbsp tahini
- 1 lime, juiced
- 1 clove garlic, minced
- 2 tbsp green onions, chopped
- 2 tbsp mint, chopped

Season the chicken: Combine cumin, paprika, allspice, turmeric, oregano, garlic powder, cinnamon, chili flake, cayenne, 1/2 tsp kosher salt and 1/2 tsp ground black pepper in a small bowl and mix thoroughly. Cut chicken into large pieces. Pour 4 tbsp olive oil over chicken pieces and combine with the spice blend. If you have time to marinate the chicken for an hour or so, do that.

Cook the chicken: Preheat oven to 400F. Line a rimmed baking sheet with foil. Bake the chicken for 15 minutes. Let it cool a bit. After chicken cools enough to handle, slice thinly and saute over high with 1 tbsp olive oil in batches - don't overcrowd the pan. Fry until the smaller pieces of chicken are brown and crispy, about 3-5 minutes.

Make the tabbouleh: In a medium bowl, stir together the cous cous, 1 tbsp of olive oil and lemon juice. Pour boiling water over the couscous and cover the bowl. Let stand for 15 minutes. Combine the cooked cous cous with the chopped vegetables and herbs. Season with salt and pepper. Taste, adjust lemon juice and olive oil if needed.

Make the sauce: Combine the yogurt, tahini, lime juice, garlic, green onions and mint in a medium bowl. If you like add 1-2 tbsp of water to thin the sauce down a bit.

Feeling kinda happy.
Peanut lime sugar snap peas

I like to pretend this is pad thai. It's not, obviously, but it has some of the fresh flavors I love about pad thai - crunchy peanuts, a little umami flavor from the fish sauce, fresh lime juice and cilantro.

MAKES 2-4 SERVINGS IN ABOUT 20 MINUTES

- 2 tsp vegetable oil
- 1 lb snap peas, ends trimmed
- 2 cloves garlic, finely chopped
- 1/4 tsp chili flakes
- 1/4 cup roasted peanuts, chopped
- 1/2 cup fresh cilantro, chopped
- 1 lime, juice and zest
- splash of fish sauce
- salt and pepper, to taste

Cook the sugar snaps: In a large skillet, heat vegetable oil over high heat. Add in snap peas and sauté over high heat for 3-4 minutes, until they are tender, but still crisp. Add in garlic and chili flakes and sauté another 30 seconds or so, until the garlic is fragrant, being sure to keep the pan moving / constantly stirring so the garlic doesn't burn.

Toss it together: Place the snap peas in a bowl and toss in the chopped peanuts, chopped cilantro and the zest from the lime. Add in the juice from 1/2 the lime and a splash of fish sauce. Taste and adjust seasonings - salt, pepper, more lime juice, more fish sauce, etc. Garnish with additional cilantro and chopped peanuts, if desired.

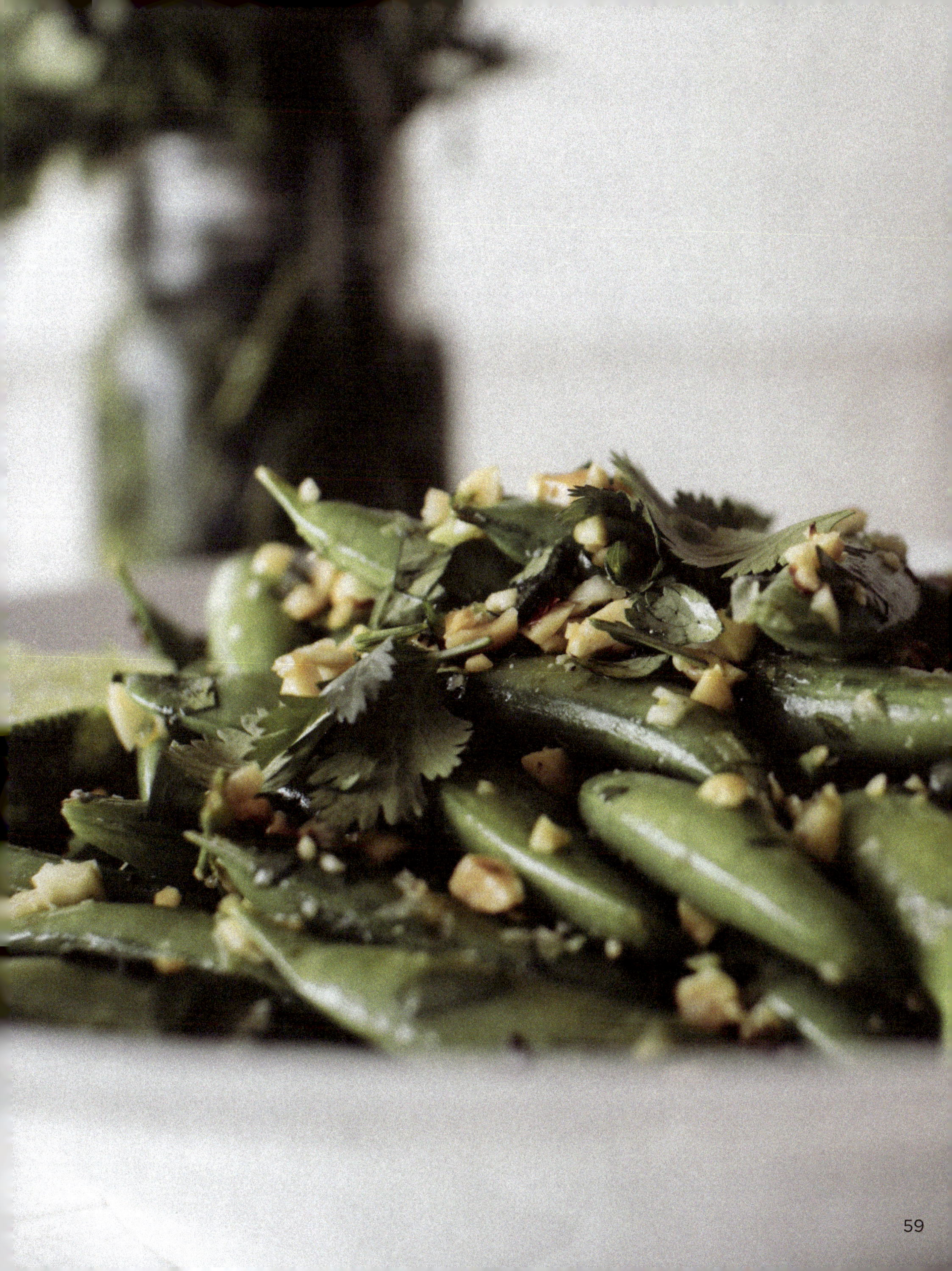

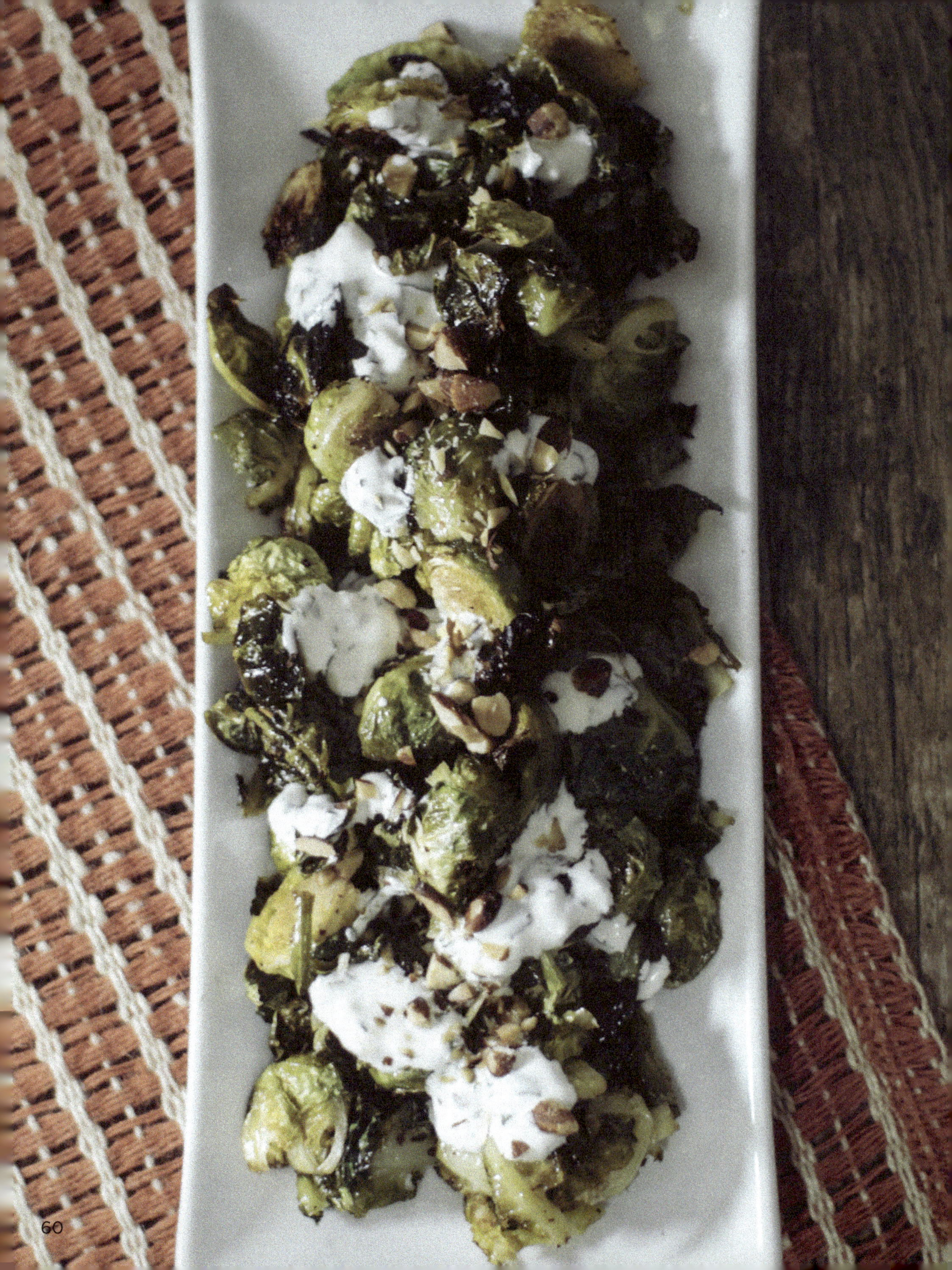

Feeling kinda happy.
Roasted brussels sprouts with garlic tahini

I love roasted brussels sprouts. I love shaking them up half way through cooking to break up the little leaves so they get extraly crunchy - the little bits get brown and crisp up like tiny brussels sprout potato chips.

MAKES 4 SERVINGS IN ABOUT 45 MINUTES

for the brussels sprouts

1 lb brussels sprouts, trimmed and halved if large

2-3 tbsp olive oil

1 tsp flaky sea salt

1/4 tsp chili flakes, more to taste

1/2 lemon, juiced

for the garlic tahini

1/2 cup labneh or Greek yogurt

2 tbsp tahini

1 clove garlic, minced

2 tbsp chopped parsley

1/2 lemon, juice and zest

sea salt and pepper

chopped almonds, for garnish

Roast the sprouts: Preheat oven to 400F. Trim any hard ends and remove any yellow leaves from the sprouts. You want them to be all about the same size, so halve any large sprouts and leave the little ones whole. Place sprouts in a baking dish. Drizzle with olive oil. Add about half of the sea salt and the chili flakes. Toss to coat.

Roast for 35-40 minutes, stirring after 20 minutes to make sure all the sprouts get equally browned and crispy. Sprinkle with remaining salt, give it a squeeze of 1/2 a lemon.

Make the sauce: While the brussels cook, combine labneh, tahini, garlic, parsley, lemon juice and zest in a small bowl. Stir to combine. Add water to desired consistency; I added about 1/4 cup of water. Drizzle over brussels sprouts and sprinkle almonds over top.

Feeling kinda happy.

Roasted salmon with baby broccoli

This is a great sheet pan meal. The broccoli and salmon cook while you make the gremolata (pg. 09), and there's only one pan to clean.

MAKES 2 SERVINGS IN ABOUT 25 MINUTES

1/2 cup panko breadcrumbs

olive oil

1/4 cup parmesan cheese

1 lb baby broccoli

salt and pepper

2 salmon fillets

2 tsp creole seasoning, more to taste

1 batch of Smoked Almond Gremolata (pg. 09)

Toast the panko: Preheat oven to 400F. In a small pan, heat about 1 tbsp of olive oil over medium high heat. Add in panko and cook, swirling the pan around, until browned and toasty. Season with salt and pepper. Let cool slightly, then mix with parmesan cheese and set aside.

Roast the baby broccoli: Place baby broccoli on a foil-lined sheet pan and drizzle with olive oil, season with salt and pepper. Toss to coat. Roast for 10 minutes.

Roast the salmon: Remove the baby broccoli from the oven and move to one side of the sheet pan. Place salmon on sheet pan and season with creole seasoning. Roast for about 12 minutes, until salmon is at desired doneness.

Top baby broccoli with toasted parmesan panko. Top salmon with smoked almond gremolata.

63

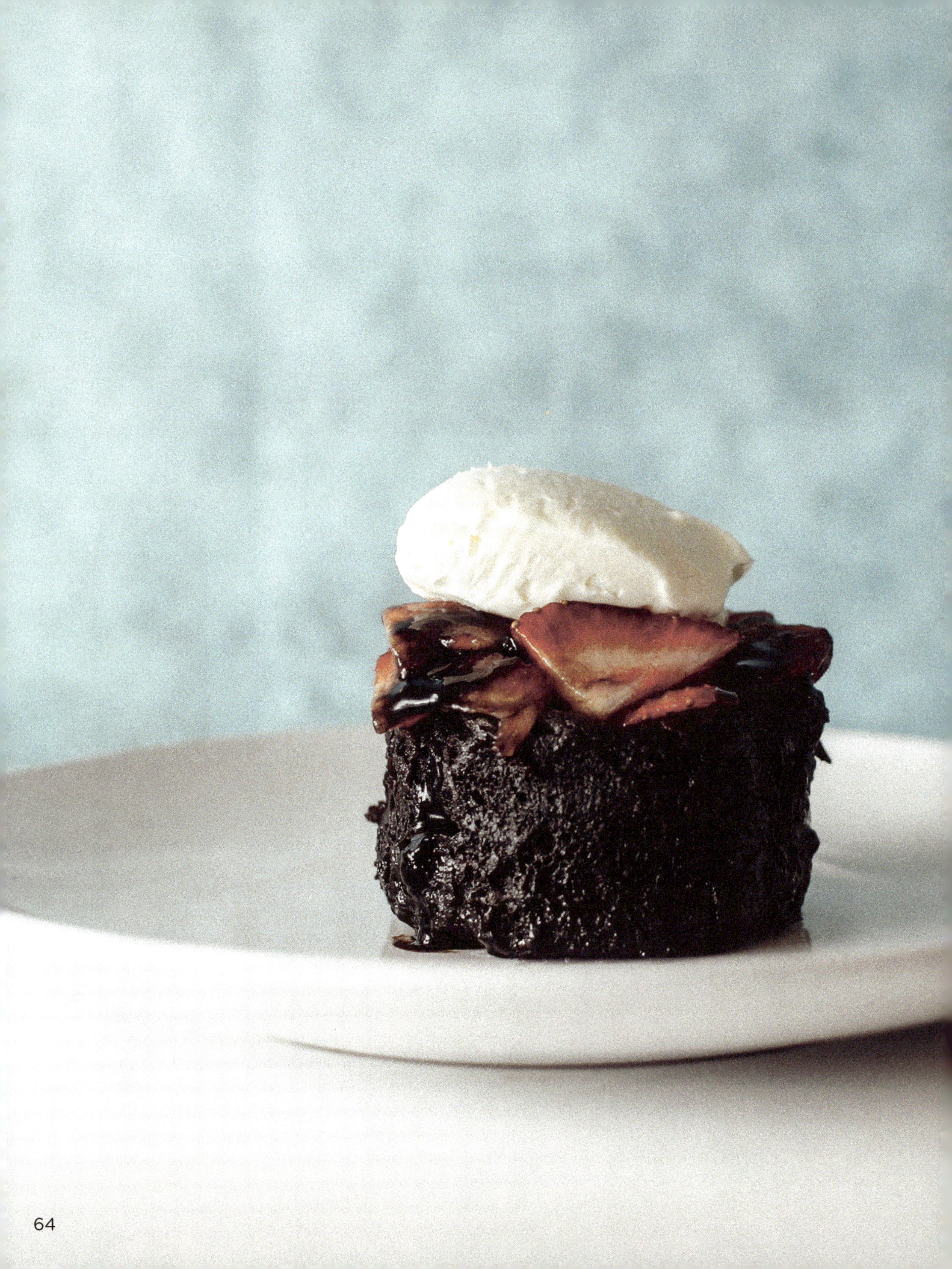

Feeling kinda happy.

$20,000 chocolate cake

Once upon a time, I was on a show called Food Fighters on NBC, where I competed against 5 professional chefs for money. This recipe won me $20,000, and I made it in a microwave LOLHOW.

MAKES 6 SERVINGS IN ABOUT 12 MINUTES

for the strawberries

1/2 pint strawberries, hulled and sliced

2 tbsp balsamic vinegar

freshly ground black pepper

1 tbsp sugar, more to taste

for the whipped cream

3 tbsp heavy cream

4 oz mascarpone

1 tbsp sugar

2-3 drops rose water to taste

for the cake

1/2 cup flour

1/2 cup sugar

1/4 cup dark cocoa powder

1 pinch flaky sea salt (like Maldon)

2 eggs

6 tbsp milk

6 tbsp vegetable oil

1/2 tsp vanilla extract

1/4 tsp espresso powder

6 chocolate truffles (like Lindt)

Marinate the strawberries: Cut berries in half lengthwise, then into slices. Add balsamic vinegar, sugar, pepper. Adjust sugar and pepper to taste. Set aside.

Make the whipped cream: Whip mascarpone and heavy cream together until well mixed. Add sugar and rose water. Whip until thickened, about 2 minutes, or to desired consistency.

Make the cake: Whisk together flour, sugar, cocoa powder and sea salt. Add in eggs, milk, oil, vanilla extract and espresso powder and mix well. Divide batter evenly between six small ramekins, leaving about 1/4" of room at the top, and place a single chocolate truffle in the middle of each. Microwave for 30 seconds. Cake should rise over the top of the ramekin slightly. If the middle still feels wet, microwave in additional 15 second spurts until cooked through.

Top cakes with sliced strawberries and some of the balsamic sauce, followed by a dollop of whipped mascarpone cream.

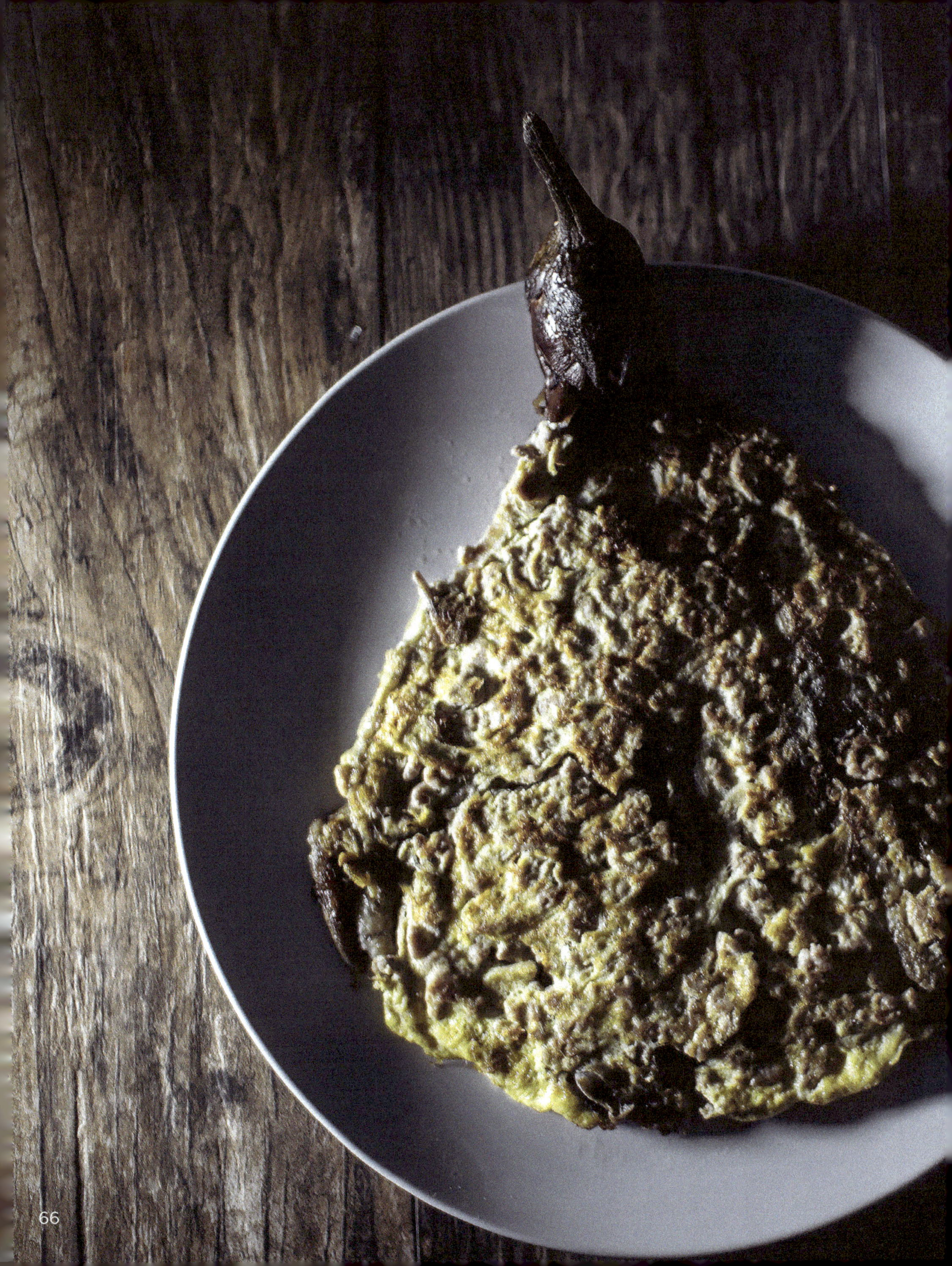

LONELY

Listen. Give me all the comfort foods now and immediately. My insides want to be warm and cozy. Specifically, I want the Filipino classics and piles of hot rice. It's not the prettiest food, but it sure is the comfortiest.

Arroz caldo with chicken chicharon (pg. 69)

Chicken kare-kare (pg. 70)

Eggplant omelette (tortang talong) (pg. 73)

Corned beef and rice (pg. 74)

Pork belly sisig (pg. 77)

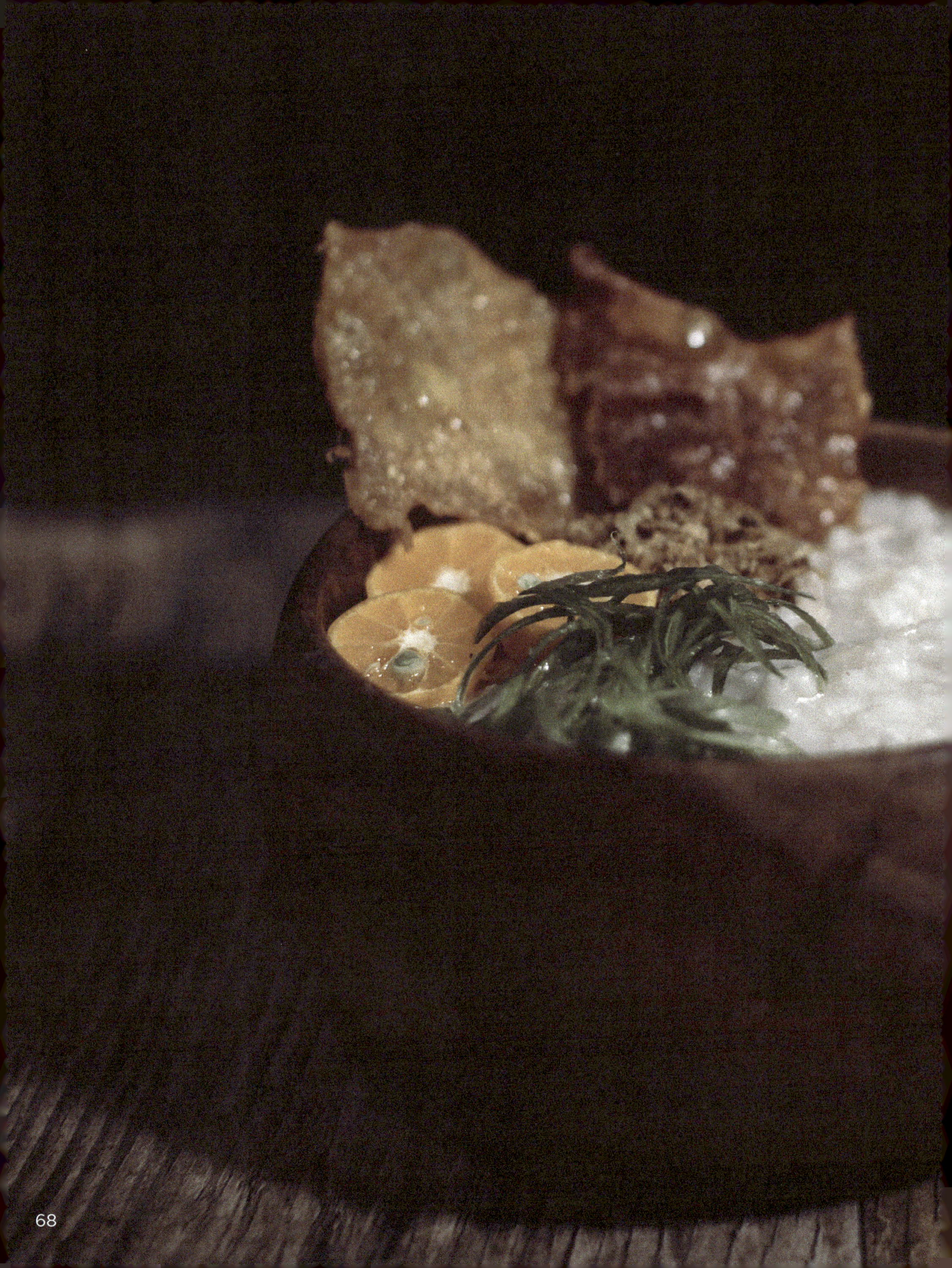

Feeling kinda lonely.

Arroz caldo with chicken chicharon

It's a rice porridge, full of chicken and comfort. Baking the chicken skin into chicharon might be the best thing I've ever done with my life. It's like chicken potato chips!

MAKES 6 SERVINGS IN ABOUT 1 HOUR 15 MINUTES

- 2 tbsp vegetable oil
- 2 cloves garlic, chopped
- 1 medium onion, chopped
- 2 thumbs of ginger, peeled and julienned
- 2 tbsp fish sauce
- 4 chicken thighs, bone-in, skin removed and reserved
- 1 chicken bouillon cube
- 8 cups water
- 1 1/2 cups uncooked rice
- fried shallots
- chopped green onions
- calamansi or lemon slices

Make the rice: In a dutch oven, add oil over medium-high heat. Saute garlic, onion and ginger until fragrant, about a minute. Add in fish sauce and rice and cook a couple more minutes. Add in chicken thighs, chicken bouillon and water. Bring to a boil, then reduce heat to a simmer. Cook, stirring occasionally to make sure rice isn't sticking to the bottom of the pot. Cook until porridge is creamy, about an hour. Taste, and add more fish sauce if needed.

Make the chicken chicharon: Preheat oven to 350F. Line a rimmed baking sheet with parchment paper and lay the chicken skins down, stretching them out so they're completely flat. Season with a good pinch of salt. Cover the chicken skins with another sheet of parchment paper, and place a baking sheet on top. This will prevent the skins from curling up. Bake for 45 minutes, or until golden and crispy.

Serve arroz caldo with fried shallots, chopped green onions and calamansi. Top with a chicharon.

Feeling kinda lonely.

Chicken kare-kare

Kare-kare is a traditional Filipino dish, usually made with oxtails. I don't always want to wait for oxtails to cook, so this is a quicker chicken version of this rich peanut butter-based stew. Serve it with piles of hot white rice.

MAKES 6 SERVINGS IN ABOUT 1 HOUR

---

3 tbsp vegetable oil

2 lbs chicken thighs, boneless and skinless

1 head garlic, peeled and cloves crushed

1 onion, sliced

2" of ginger, cut into strips

4 cups chicken broth or stock

1 tbsp annatto seed powder

1 cup natural peanut butter

1/2 cup toasted ground rice (see notes)

4 medium size eggplants, cut on the bias in 2" pieces

1 bunch (1/2 lb) long beans, cut 2 inches pieces

1 can coconut milk

1 tbsp patis, more to taste

8 pieces baby bok choy

bagoong (shrimp paste) for serving

Brown the chicken: In a large pot, heat vegetable oil. Working in batches, add the chicken to the pot and brown on both sides, about 4-5 minutes. Remove the chicken and set aside.

Add in the broth and seasonings: Add the garlic, onion and ginger to the pot, adding additional oil if necessary, and saute until fragrant, about 5 minutes. Add in chicken stock and deglaze the bottom of the pan (scrape up all those delicious little brown bits). Add in annatto seed powder. Add peanut butter and stir until fully incorporated. Add in ground rice and stir to incorporate. The sauce should become thick. Add in chicken, cover pot and simmer on medium heat for 10 minutes, stirring occasionally; sometimes the ground rice can get stuck to the bottom of the pan and burn.

Add in veggies: Add in long beans and eggplant. Cook an additional 15-25 minutes, until eggplant is cooked. Stir occasionally. Once eggplant is cooked through, add coconut milk and baby bok choy. Simmer until bok choy is cooked through, 5-10 minutes.

Serve with hot rice and add a side of bagoong if you want to keep it trill.

Notes: You can substitute toasted ground rice for Mama Sita's Kare-Kare Mix. Only use 1/2 cup peanut butter if you do it this way.

This is also a great way to use up veggies. Throw in whatever you have on hand.

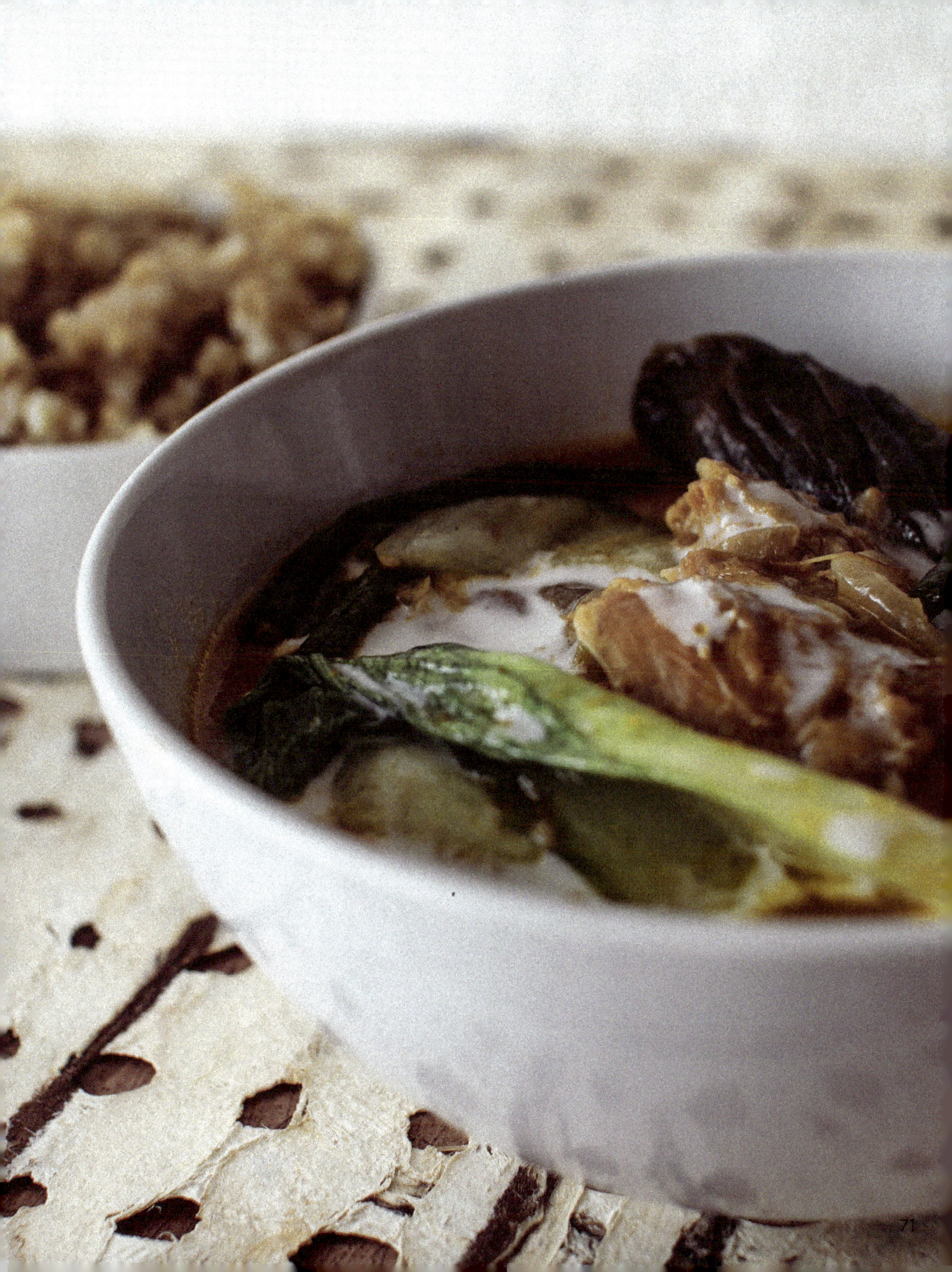

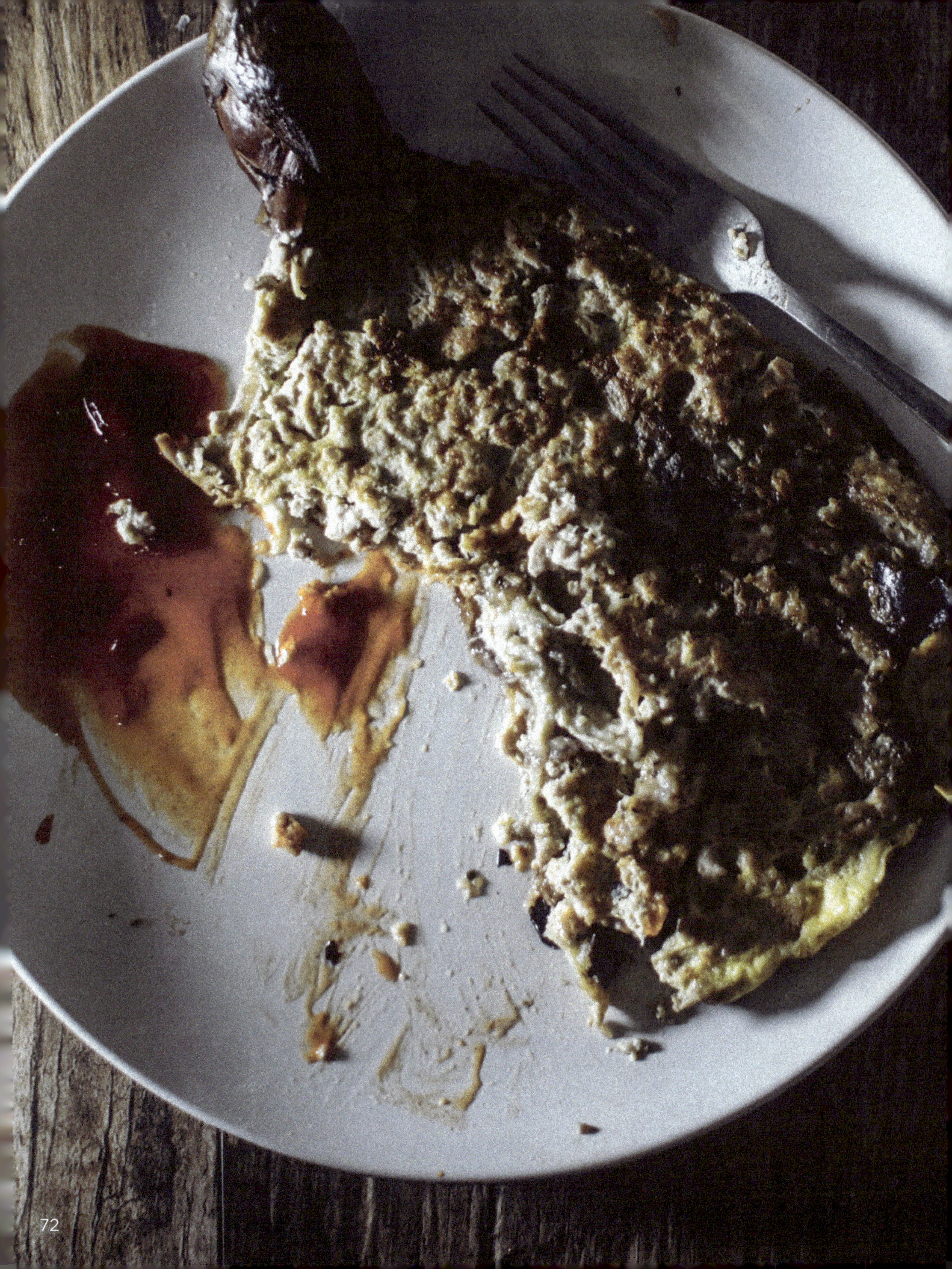

Feeling kinda lonely.

Eggplant omelette

This traditional Filipino breakfast food, also known as tortang talong, is like roasted eggplant and an omelette had a delicious baby. Serve with lots of hot white rice and spicy banana ketchup.

MAKES 4 SERVINGS IN ABOUT 45 MINUTES

- 4 Chinese eggplants
- vegetable oil
- 5-6 cloves garlic, minced
- 1 medium onion, minced
- 1 lb ground pork
- 1 tbsp soy sauce
- 1/2 tsp sesame oil
- 4 large eggs, beaten
- salt and pepper to taste
- 2 chopped green onions for garnish
- banana ketchup, for serving

Cook the eggplant: Grill or broil eggplants until skin is charred all over, turning as needed. Place charred eggplant in a bowl and cover with plastic wrap to help steam off the skin. Let cool enough to touch, then remove the charred skin, leaving the stem of the eggplant intact. Flatten the eggplant a bit and set aside.

Cook the pork: In a large skillet, heat about 1 tbsp vegetable oil over medium high heat. Add in garlic and onion and saute for a few minutes. Add in ground pork, soy sauce and sesame oil. Cook until the pork is no longer pink. Set aside and wipe out the pan. Once the mixture has cooled, combine with the beaten eggs.

Make the omelette: Place about 1 tbsp of vegetable oil in the pan and place one piece of eggplant in the pan. Top with about 1/4 of ground pork and egg mixture on top of the eggplant, more or less depending on the size, and spread it evenly. Cook for 2-3 minutes, Carefully flip the omelette, holding the stem of the eggplant and using a large spatula, and cook another 2-3 minutes.

Garnish with green onions and serve with hot white rice and banana ketchup.

Notes: You can find banana ketchup at Asian markets in the condiments section.

Feeling kinda lonely.

Corned beef and rice

Listen, I'm not big on eating canned meats, but THIS RIGHT HERE. It's pure, quick comfort. Add in some diced potatoes to make it a heartier meal, or top with an over easy egg. Or do both. Or have it plain, just like this.

MAKES 2-3 SERVINGS IN ABOUT 15 MINUTES

2 tbsp vegetable oil

1 onion, diced

2 cloves garlic, chopped

1 can corned beef

1/4 cup chopped green onions

6 cups cooked white rice

ground black pepper

Cook the corned beef: In a large skillet, heat oil over medium high heat. Add onions and garlic and sauté for about a minute. Add in corned beef and break up with a wooden spoon. Cook until heated through, about 6-8 minutes. Turn the heat to high and let the corned beef get a bit crispy in spots, if you like. Season with pepper to taste.

Serve corned beef with rice. Garnish with green onions.

Notes: Add in cooked diced potatoes or top with an over easy egg (or both!) for a heartier meal.

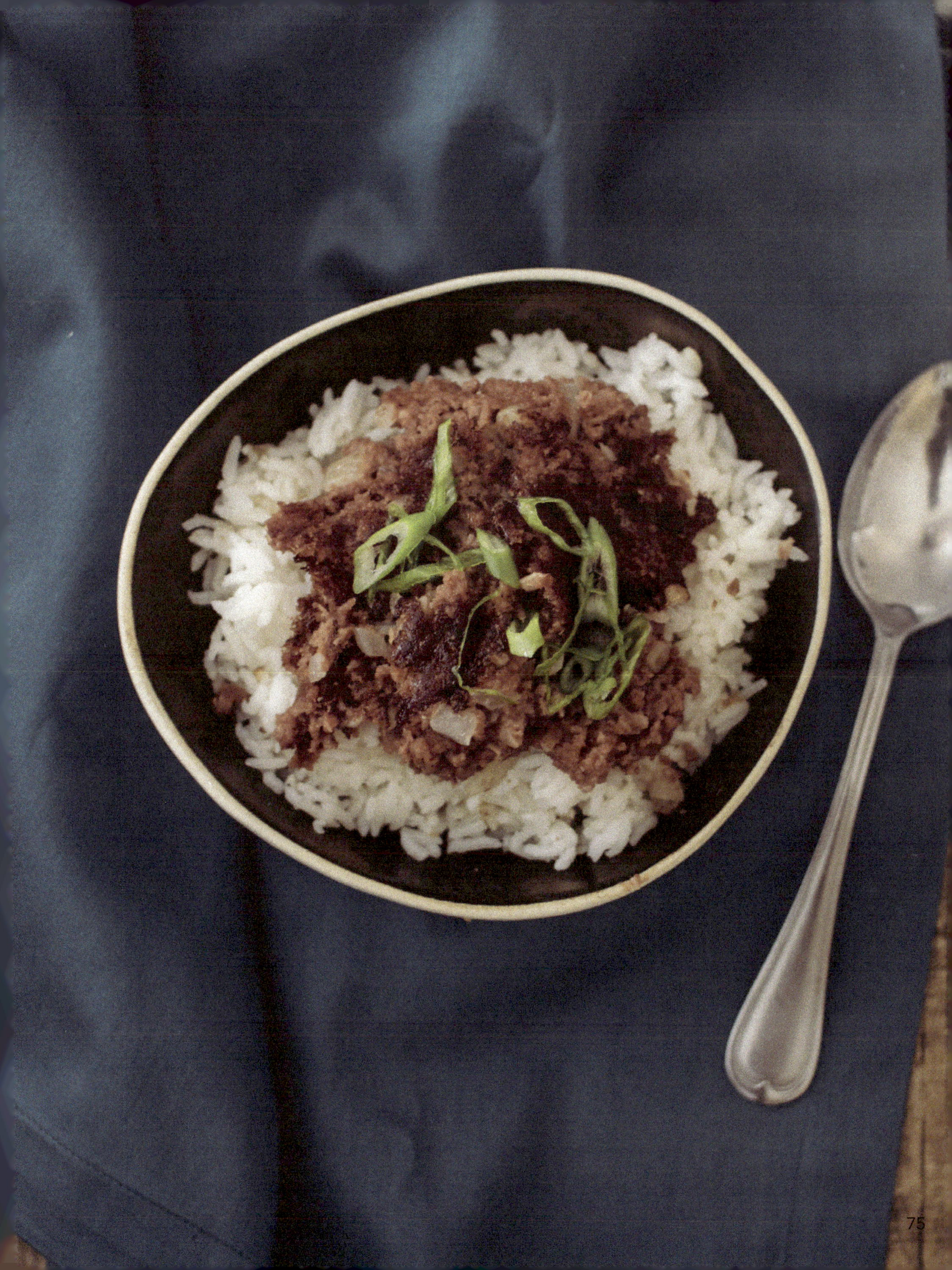

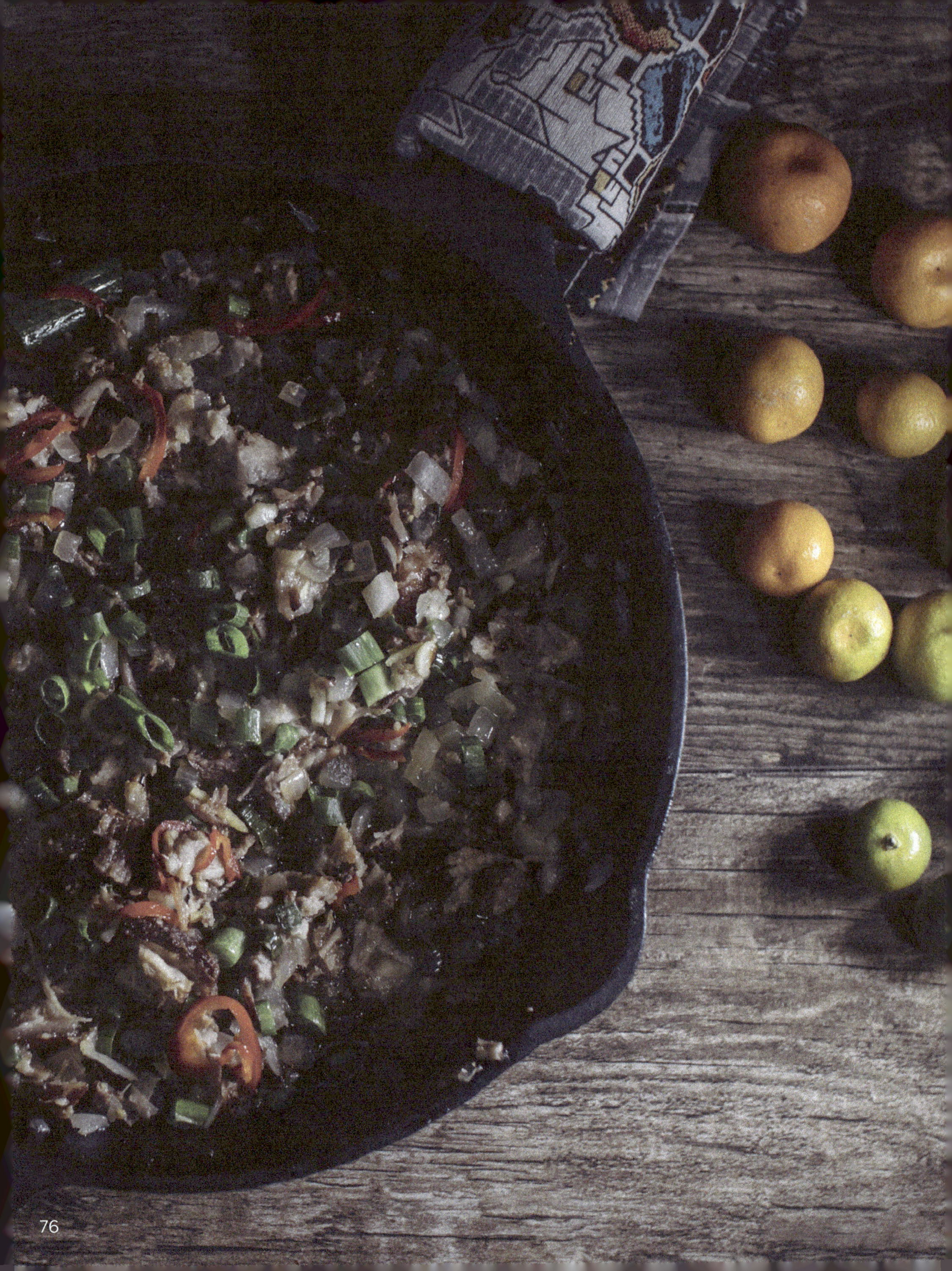

Feeling kinda lonely.
Pork belly sisig

Sisig is usually made with the head of the pig. Generally, I don't want to deal with an entire pig's head, so this is essentially cheat code sisig, using flavorful pork belly in lieu of pig ears and snouts,

MAKES 4-6 SERVINGS IN ABOUT 1 HOUR 30 MINUTES, PLUS TIME FOR COOLING

- 2 lbs pork belly, cut into ~2" chunks
- 1/2 cup soy sauce
- 1/2 cup cane or white vinegar
- 1 tbsp whole peppercorns
- 10 cloves garlic, smashed
- 1 bay leaf
- 1 tbsp vegetable oil
- 1 tbsp finely chopped ginger
- 5 cloves garlic, chopped
- 1 onion, diced
- 1-3 chopped red fresno or jalapeno chiles, to taste
- 3-4 calamansi or 1/2 lemon, more to taste
- 2 tbsp cane vinegar, more to taste
- 1-2 tbsp soy sauce, more to taste
- 1/4 cup chopped green onion, plus more for garnish

Braise the pork belly: Combine pork, soy sauce, vinegar, peppercorns, garlic and bay leaf in pressure cooker. If needed, add just enough water to cover pork belly. Bring the pressure cooker up to high pressure, then lower the heat to maintain that pressure. Cook for 30 minutes. Quick-release the pressure according to your pressure cooker's instructions. If you don't have a pressure cooker, braise in a dutch oven for about 1 1/2 hours, until meat is soft but not falling apart.

Chop the pork belly: Remove the pork belly from the pot. Reserve 1/4 cup of the cooking liquid. Crisp up the pork belly skin by either grilling, or placing on a foil-lined baking sheet and broiling, until the skin is browned and beginning to blister in spots. Let the pork belly cool, then chop into small pieces.

Season the sisig: In a large pan, add 1 tbsp vegetable oil and saute ginger, garlic, onion and chili for one minute. Add pork and saute 4-5 more minutes, until pieces have browned and gotten a bit crispy. Remove from the heat and season with calamansi, vinegar and green onion. Taste, and adjust seasonings as needed. It should be salty, sour and spicy and stick to your lips like the best lip gloss ever. Serve with rice.

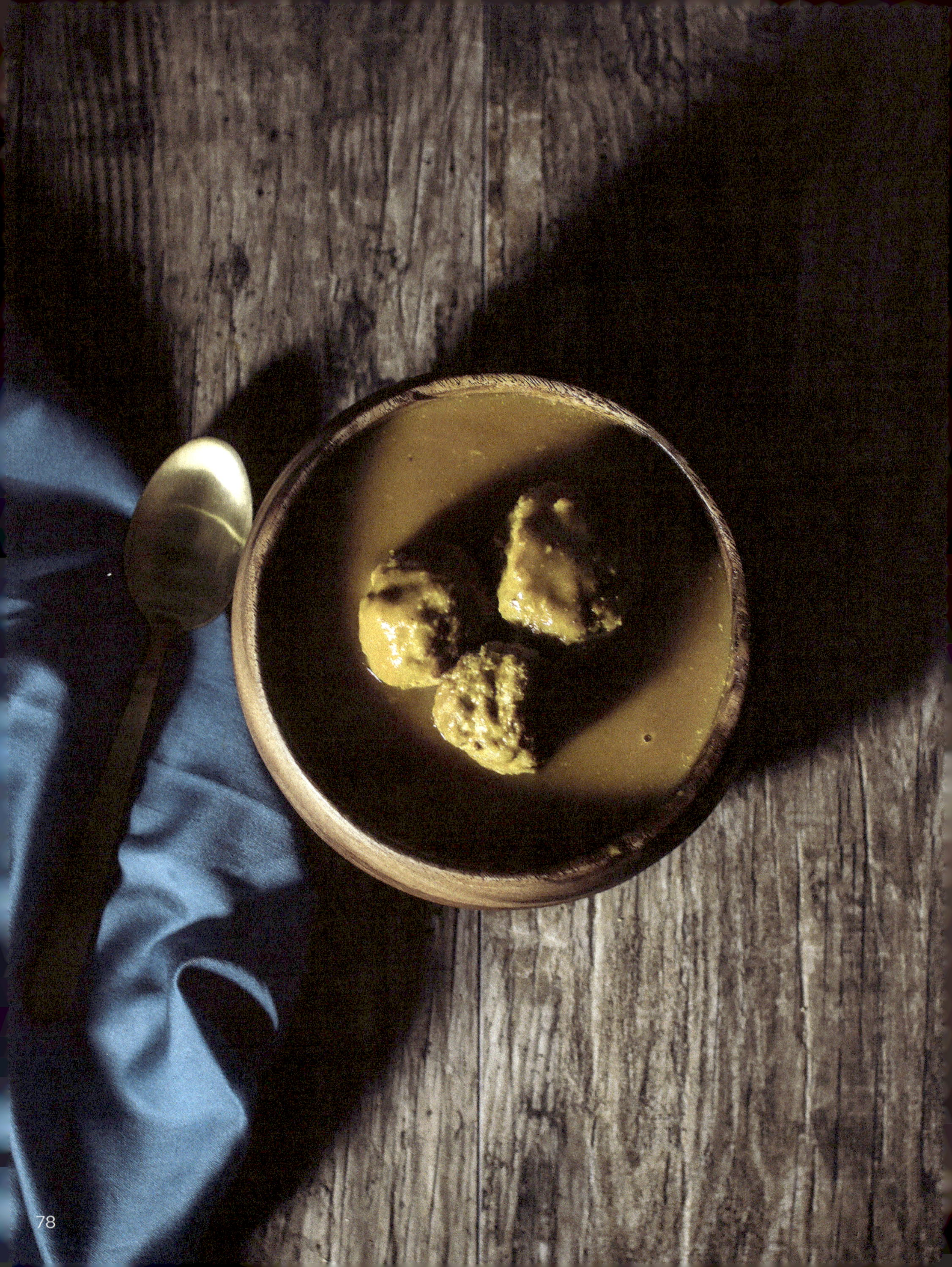

MESSY

...or petty, or generally feeling like instigating some things you know you don't need to instigate. Or maybe logging into your fake Facebook account so you can check your ex's profile because you've blocked them on your real one but you still want to see what's going on. No? Mmmkay.

I like these quick recipes to help re-focus my energy on delicious things, instead of the catastrophes I could create.

Labneh toasts (pg. 81)

Gorgonzola and bacon drop biscuits (pg. 82)

A carton soup and meatballs (pg.n 85)

Shrimp and mascarpone grits (pg. 86)

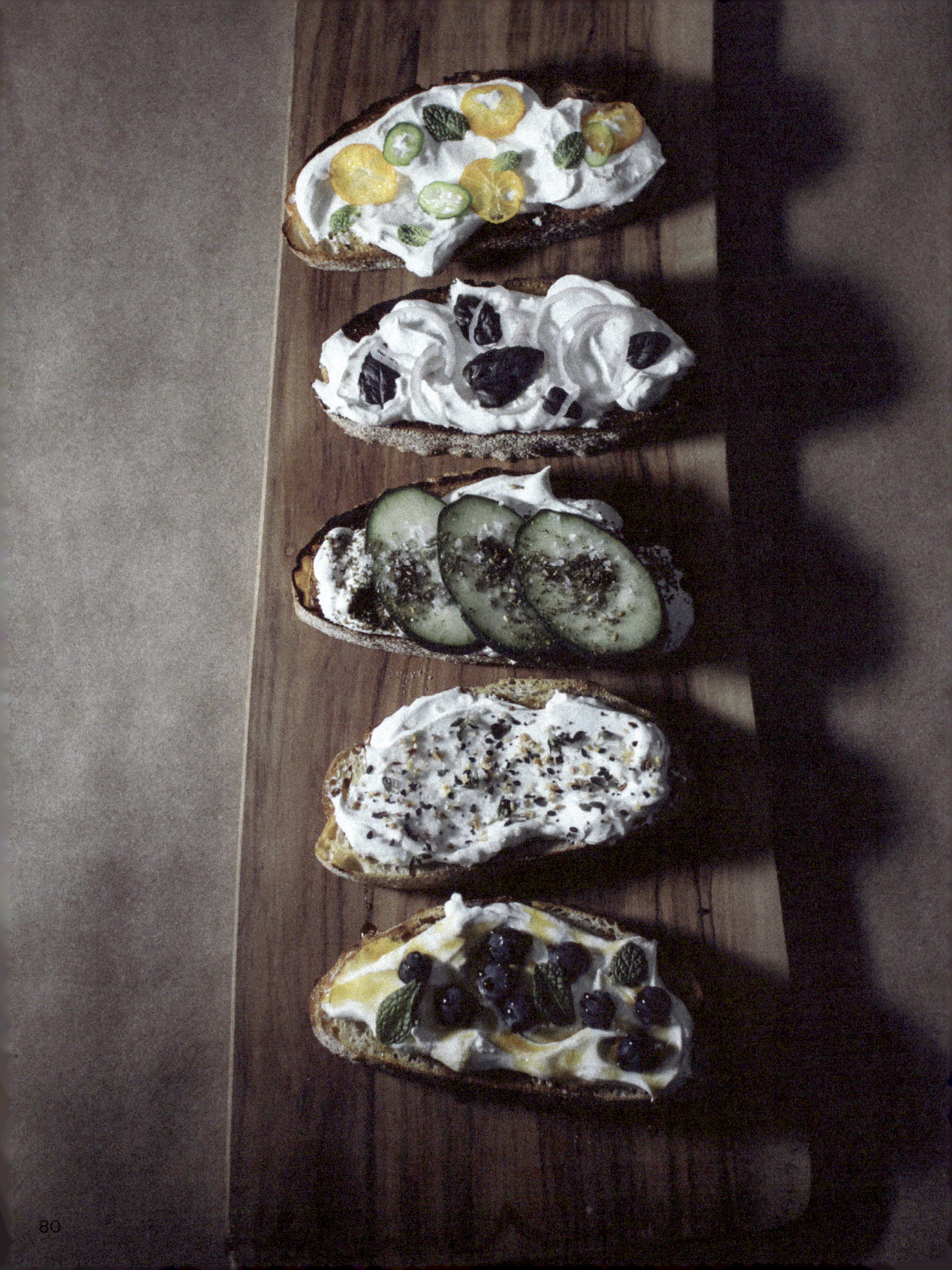

Feeling kinda messy.
Labneh toasts

It's the new avocado toast. If you've never had labneh before, meet your new favorite creamy friend. It has the richness of sour cream but the tanginess of yogurt. And, since it's cultured dairy, its chocked full of that good good that keeps your guts right.

MAKES AS MUCH AS YOU WANT IN A FEW MINUTES

French levain or sourdough bread, sliced about 1" thick

olive oil

labneh

flaky sea salt (like Maldon)

Toast the bread: Brush bread with a bit of olive oil and toast one side in a hot skillet until browned, about 2-3 minutes. Top with a spoonful of labneh and sea salt, and whatever toppings you'd like. Labneh makes everything taste good so get creative. Here are some of my favorite combinations:

Zaatar + cucumber: Sprinkle zaatar and sliced cucumbers overtop.

Shallots + maldon: Thinly sliced shallots and sea salt on top of labneh is simple and magical.

Blueberry + honey: For a sweet twist, use blueberries (or your favorite berry) with a bit of honey for a quick breakfast.

Preserved lemon + chili + mint: Savory, spicy and fresh, the preserved lemons add an bright burst of citrus and salt.

Fried mushroom + thyme: Fry sliced mushrooms in olive oil until crispy, then add a bit of fresh thyme and sea salt.

Everything bagel seasoning + capers

Feeling kinda messy.

Gorgonzola and bacon drop biscuits

If the idea of baking is intimidating, make these biscuits. No kneading, no cutting out shapes, just dump everything in a bowl, drop it on a sheet pan and bake.

MAKES 12 BISCUITS IN ABOUT 30 MINUTES

- 2 1/2 cups all-purpose flour
- 2 1/2 tsp baking powder
- 2 tsp sugar
- 3/4 tsp baking soda
- 1 tsp salt
- 8 tbsp cold unsalted butter, cut into cubes
- 1 cup crumbled Gorgonzola
- 3 green onions, finely chopped
- 7 slices bacon, cooked crispy and chopped
- 1 cup milk

Mix the dough: Preheat oven to 450°F. Whisk together flour, baking powder, sugar, baking soda, and salt in a bowl. Using your fingertips, blend the butter into the flour until the mixture resembles small peas. Stir in blue cheese, chopped bacon and green onions. Add milk and stir just until the mixture comes together; you don't want to overwork the dough.

Bake the biscuits: Drop dough in 12 equal mounds, about 1-2" apart, onto a large parchment-lined baking sheet. Bake on the middle rack of the oven until golden and baked through, about 16 to 20 minutes.

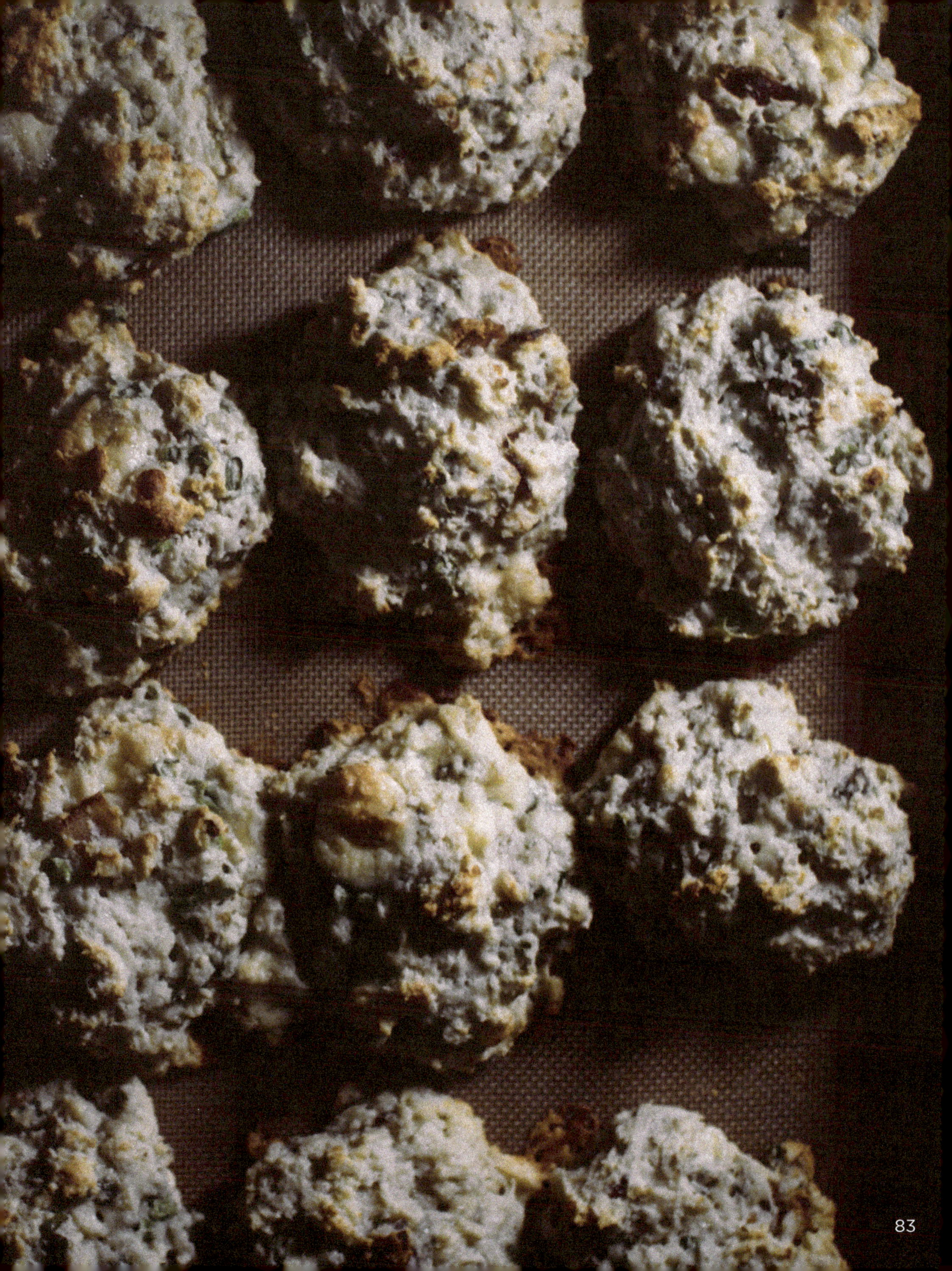

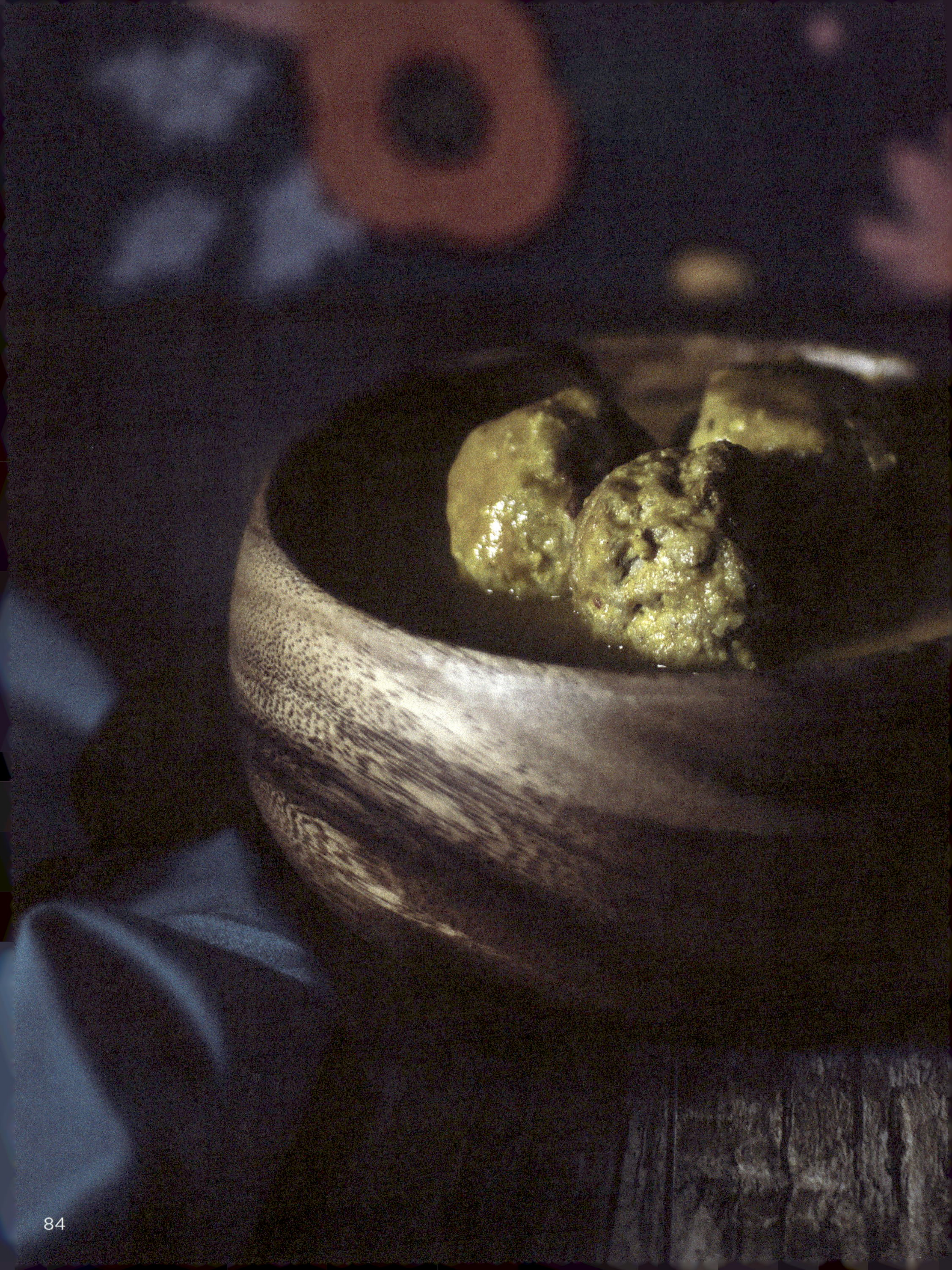

Feeling kinda messy.

A carton of soup and meatballs

Trader Joe's has lovely soups that come in cartons. I usually keep a couple of those on hand for times when I don't necessarily feel like cooking a whole meal from scratch. Add in one of the meatball variations below and you've got quite a filling soup. It's also great over quinoa or rice.

MAKES 4 SERVINGS IN ABOUT 30 MINUTES

- 1 lb ground meat (pork, chicken, turkey, etc)
- 2 cloves garlic, minced
- 1/4 tsp chili flakes
- 1/4 cup panko
- 1 egg
- 1 tsp salt
- vegetable oil
- 1 32 oz carton of soup of your choice

Make the meatballs: Combine ground meat, garlic, chili flakes, panko, egg and any herbs and spices (see combinations below) that work best with whatever soup you have. Form into meatballs, about 1" wide.

Cook the meatballs: Heat a medium pot over medium high heat and add in about 1 tbsp of vegetable oil. Brown meatballs on all sides, in batches if needed, about 10 minutes. Once browned, add the soup and simmer over medium heat until warm and meatballs are cooked through, about 10-15 minutes.

Meatball variations

Asian: Add in 1 tbsp of chopped ginger and 1/2 tbsp sesame oil. This version is great with carrot ginger soup.

Five Spice: Add in 1 tsp Chinese five spice powder, 1 minced clove of garlic and 1 tbsp of chopped ginger.

Italian: Add in 1/2 cup chopped fresh basil, 1/4 cup Parmesan cheese and 1 tsp dried oregano.

Moroccan: Add in 2 tsp ground cumin, 1/2 tsp cinnamon, 1/2 tsp paprika, 1/4 tsp allspice, 1/4 tsp cayenne, 1/4 tsp ground cardamom, 1/4 cup chopped mint and 1/2 cup chopped cilantro.

Middle Eastern: Add in 1/2 chop chopped parsley and 2 tbsp zaatar.

Pictured left: Carrot ginger soup with Asian turkey meatballs.

Feeling kinda messy.
Shrimp and mascarpone grits

Really, is there a situation where shrimp and grits can't make something immediately awesomer? No.

MAKES 4 SERVINGS IN ABOUT 35 MINUTES

for the bacon tomato sauce

- 3 strips bacon, roughly chopped
- 1 14.5-oz can crushed tomatoes
- 1 large shallot, peeled and halved
- 4 tbsp butter
- salt and pepper, to taste

for the grits

- 4 cups chicken broth
- 1 cup quick cooking grits
- 8 oz mascarpone

for the shrimp

- 1 lb raw shrimp, peeled and deveined
- 2 tsp creole seasoning (like Tony Chachare's)
- 1 tbsp butter
- 2 green onions, chopped, for garnish

Make the bacon tomato sauce: In a medium saucepan, saute bacon until crispy. Remove bacon with a slotted spoon and drain on paper towels. In the same pan, add tomatoes, shallot and butter. Simmer for 25 minutes. Remove from the heat and discard the shallot. Season with salt and pepper to taste.

Make the grits: In a medium pot with a lid, add 4 cups chicken broth and bring to a boil. Once boiling, reduce heat to a simmer and stir in grits. Cover, stirring occasionally, until the grits are thick, about 15 minutes. Once the grits are thick, stir in the mascarpone until well combined. Season with salt and pepper to taste and keep warm.

Make the shrimp: Season shrimp with about 1 tsp of creole seasoning. Melt butter in skillet over medium high heat. Fry shrimp until opaque and cooked through, about 1 minute per side.

Place grits in a bowl and top with shrimp and tomato sauce; garnish with crumbled bacon and green onions.

87

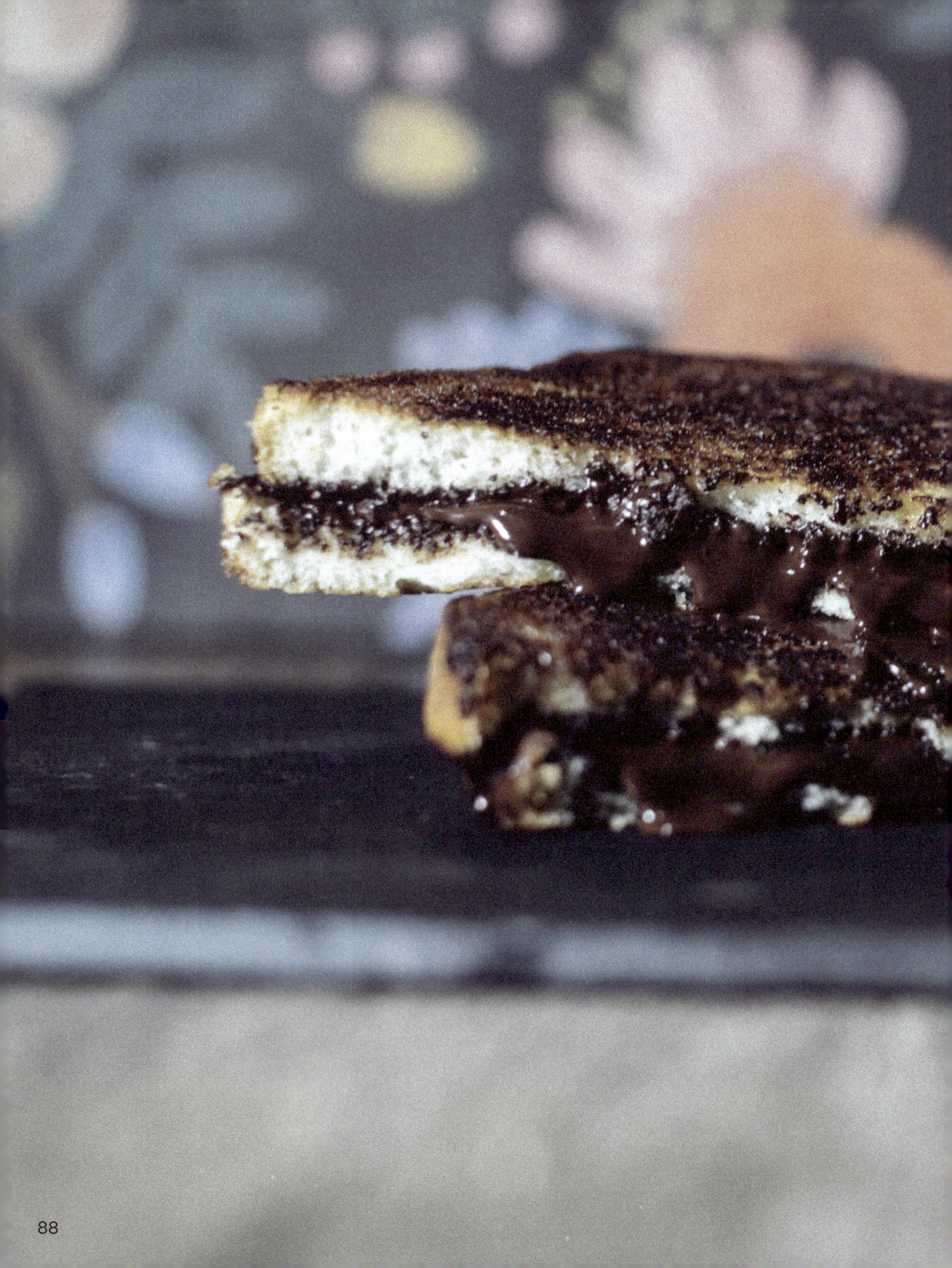

SAD AF

Oh look, recipes I can make while crying.

I'm sad as fuck.

Sesame beef and spinach bowl (pg. 91)

Chicken adobo (pg. 92)

Spinach soup (pg. 95)

BBQ shrimp toast (pg. 96)

Chocolate sandwich (pg. 99)

90

Feeling kinda sad.
Sesame beef and spinach bowl

This comes together SO quick. Lifehack: "shabu-shabu" cut ribeye from the Asian market is the perfect cut for this..

MAKES 4 SERVINGS IN ABOUT 30 MINUTES

- 1 lb boneless ribeye, thinly sliced
- 1 1/2 tbsp sake
- 1" ginger, peeled and minced
- 3 cloves garlic, minced; divided
- 1/4 tsp chili flakes, more to taste
- 2 tsp cornstarch
- 3 tbsp soy sauce
- 3 tsp sugar
- 2 1/2 tbsp sesame oil
- 24 oz baby spinach
- salt and pepper
- 2 tbsp furikake or toasted sesame seeds, for garnish
- 6 cups cooked white rice

Season the beef: In a bowl, combine the beef, sake, ginger, half of the garlic and the chili flakes and mix. Add the cornstarch and stir to coat.

Mix the sauce: In a another small bowl, stir together 1/4 cup water, 3 tbsp soy sauce, 3 tsp sugar and 1/2 tbsp of sesame oil.

Cook the spinach: In a large skillet, heat 1 tbsp of sesame oil over high heat. Add in remaining garlic and the baby spinach. Saute until spinach has wilted, about 2-3 minutes. Season with salt and pepper and set aside. Wipe out the pan.

Cook the beef: Add in remaining 1 tbsp of sesame oil and the beef. Stir-fry the beef over high heat until almost cooked through, then add the soy sauce mixture. Bring it all to a boil, stirring constantly until the sauce thickens and coats the meat nicely.

Serve spinach and beef over hot white rice. Garnish with furikake.

Feeling kinda sad.

Chicken adobo

Really, truly, this is the ultimate Filipino comfort food. Everyone has their own version and everyone's mom makes it the best. My version uses coconut milk to add a bit of richness to the sauce, because I mostly eat sauce and rice and the chicken is just nice to have.

MAKES 4 SERVINGS IN ABOUT 45 MINUTES

- 2 lbs of chicken thighs; skin reserved to make chicharons
- 1 tbsp vegetable oil
- 2" piece of ginger, peeled and julienned
- 10 cloves garlic, peeled and smashed
- 1/4 tsp chili flakes
- 1 14oz can of coconut milk
- 1/3 cup soy sauce
- 2/3 cup cane vinegar
- 4 bay leaves
- 1 tbsp whole peppercorns
- 1 onion, sliced 1/8" thick
- 6 cups cooked white rice

Brown the chicken: In a large pot, heat vegetable oil over medium heat. Saute ginger, smashed garlic and chili flakes in oil until fragrant, about a minute. Add in the chicken and brown on all sides, about 5 minutes.

Add the liquids and spices: Add in coconut milk, soy sauce, vinegar, bay leaves and peppercorns and bring to a simmer. Cover and simmer for 20 minutes. Add in onions and simmer another 10 minutes, until chicken is tender and onions have softened.

Serve over hot rice topped with the sauce and onions from the pot.

Optional step: Remove the chicken skins and make chicken chicharons for garnish; see the Arroz caldo recipe on page 69.

93

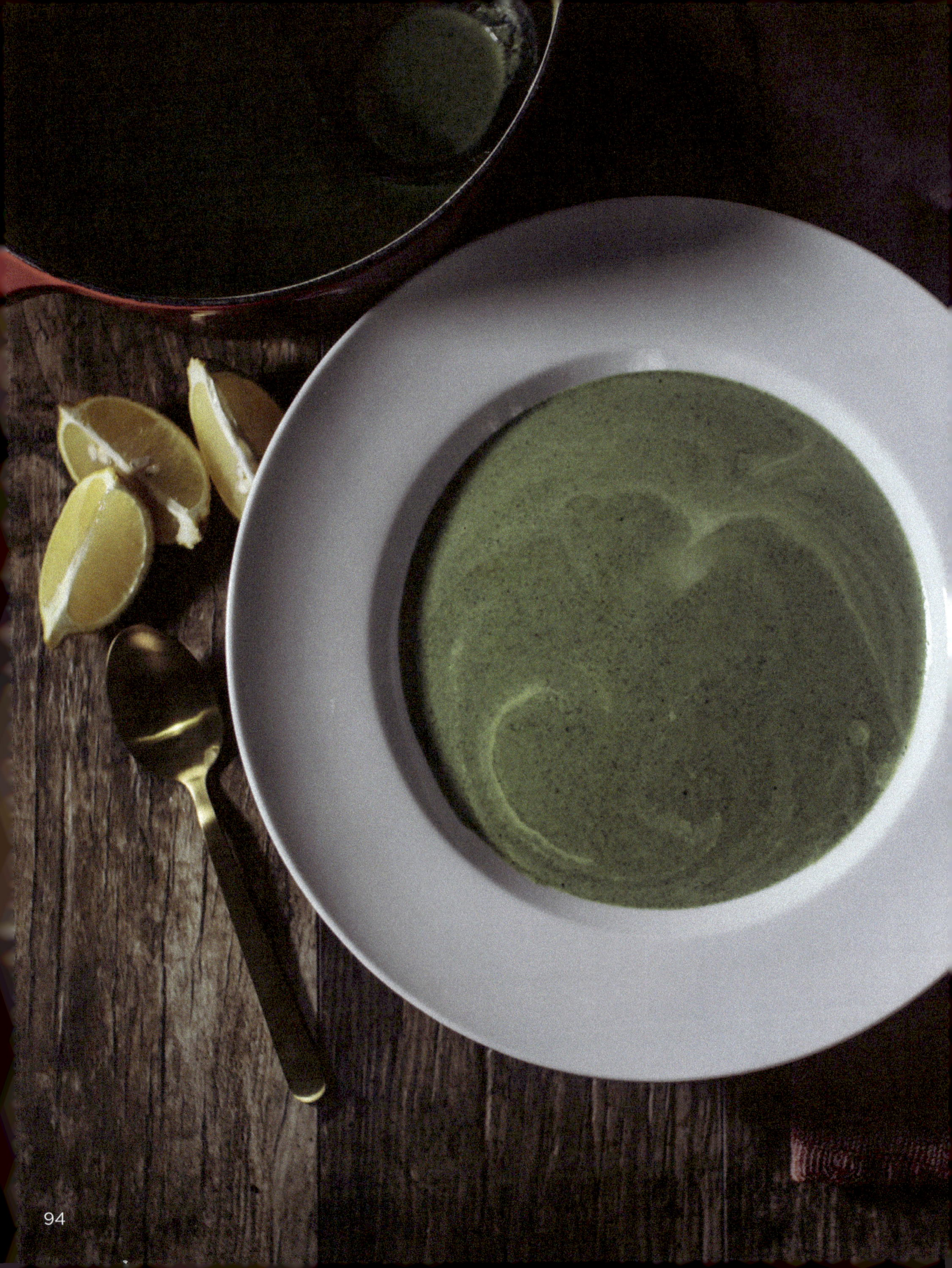

Feeling kinda sad.

Spinach soup

Spinach and coconut milk come together with chilies and spices to make a super quick soup you can totes cry into. This is also a great recipe to break out for your vegan friends.

MAKES 4 SERVINGS IN ABOUT 45 MINUTES

---

2 tbsp coconut oil

1/2 cup finely chopped onion

1 or 2 Serrano chillies, minced; use 1 and remove seeds for less spice

2 garlic cloves, minced

1" chunk of ginger, minced

1 1/2 tsp ground cumin

1/2 tsp ground coriander

1/4 tsp ground black pepper

1/2 tsp ground turmeric

2 bay leaves

2 cups vegetable stock

1 - 13.5 oz can coconut milk

3 cups packed fresh spinach leaves

1/2 cup coconut cream

sea salt

lemon wedges, for serving

Start the broth: In a heavy bottomed pot, add coconut oil over medium heat. Add the grated garlic, ginger and Serrano chillies. Let cook for about a minute, until fragrant. Add the chopped onions and saute until soft and translucent, about 3-5 minutes. Add the spices and saute for another 30 seconds. Reduce the heat to minimum and add the vegetable stock, bay leaves and coconut milk. Let simmer on low heat for 30 minutes.

Add the spinach: Remove the bay leaves from the stock. Add the spinach and bring to a simmer. Simmer, uncovered, until spinach is cooked through, about 5 minutes.

Add the cream: Reduce the heat to low and add the in the coconut cream and salt to taste. Simmer for two minutes.

Blend it together: Remove from heat and blend soup with an immersion / stick blender until desired consistency. If using a food processor or blender to puree, let soup cool down and process in batches. Adjust salt and pepper to taste.

Serve warm with lemon wedges and garnish with chili flakes.

Feeling kinda sad.
BBQ shrimp toast

I'm not quite sure how this became known as "BBQ", but I had this dish for the first time in New Orleans and it immediately lifted my spirits to new heights. Shrimp and half a pound of butter will do that.

MAKES 2 SERVINGS AS AN APPETIZER IN ABOUT 45 MINUTES

for the shrimp

- 10 jumbo (21/25 ct) shrimp, tail-on and deveined; shells reserved for shrimp broth
- 1 bay leaf
- 5 whole peppercorns
- 1 tbsp olive oil
- 2 tsp creole seasoning (like Tony Chachare's)
- 3/4 cup unsalted butter
- 2 cloves garlic, chopped
- 1/2 cup white wine
- 1 cup shrimp broth
- 2 tbsp Worcestershire Sauce
- 2 tbsp lemon juice
- 5 dashes Crystal Hot Sauce
- 2 tbsp chopped parsley
- salt and pepper
- 2 stalks green onions, chopped

for the toast

- 4 tbsp unsalted butter
- 1 clove garlic, finely chopped
- 2 tbsp chopped parsley
- salt & pepper
- 2 slices of French levain bread or sourdough, cut 1 1/2" thick slices

Make a quick shrimp broth: In a small saucepan, add shrimp shells, 2 cups of water, a few parsley stems, a bay leaf and a few peppercorns and simmer for 15 minutes. Strain and discard the solids.

Cook the shrimp: Add olive oil to a pan over medium-high heat. Add in shrimp and season with creole seasoning. Add in 2 tbsp of butter and garlic and sauté shrimp for about a minute. Add in the white wine and deglaze the pan. Reduce the liquid by about half, then remove the shrimp from the pan.

Make the sauce: Add in shrimp stock, Worcestershire, lemon juice, and hot sauce. Simmer, then reduce by 3/4, about 12-15 minutes. Turn the heat to low and slowly whisk in the remaining butter into the sauce until smooth and luscious. Add in parsley and adjust salt and pepper to taste.

Make the toast: While the sauce is reducing, get started on the toast. Preheat oven to 350F. Melt together butter, garlic, parsley and salt & pepper to taste in a small saucepan. Brush bread slices on both sides with butter and toast @ 350F for 8-10 minutes, until golden brown.

Top the toasted bread with the shrimp, douse with sauce and garnish with green onions.

Notes: Don't use a flimsy bread with this dish. It needs to be thick and dense to soak up all the delicious sauce.

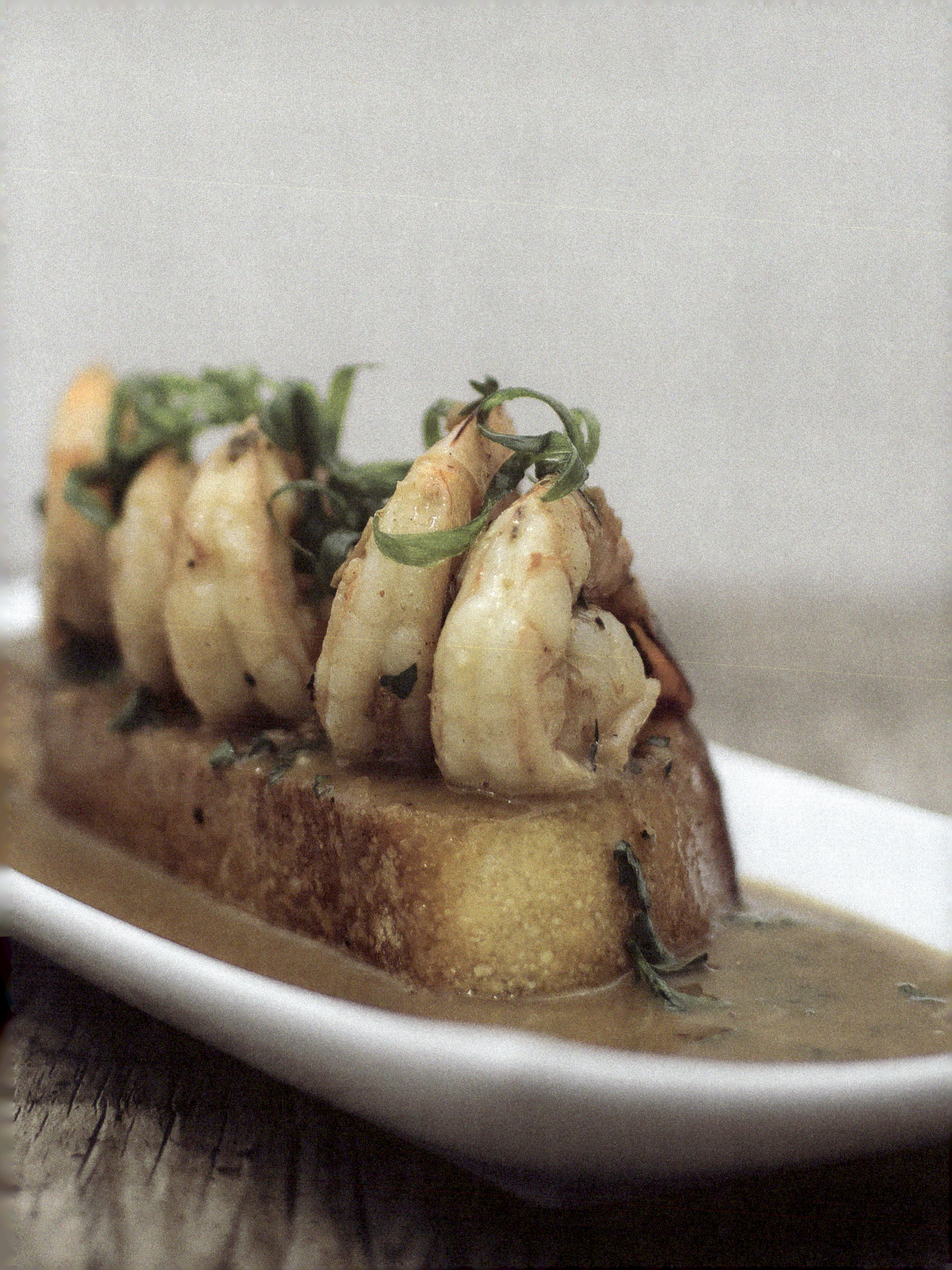

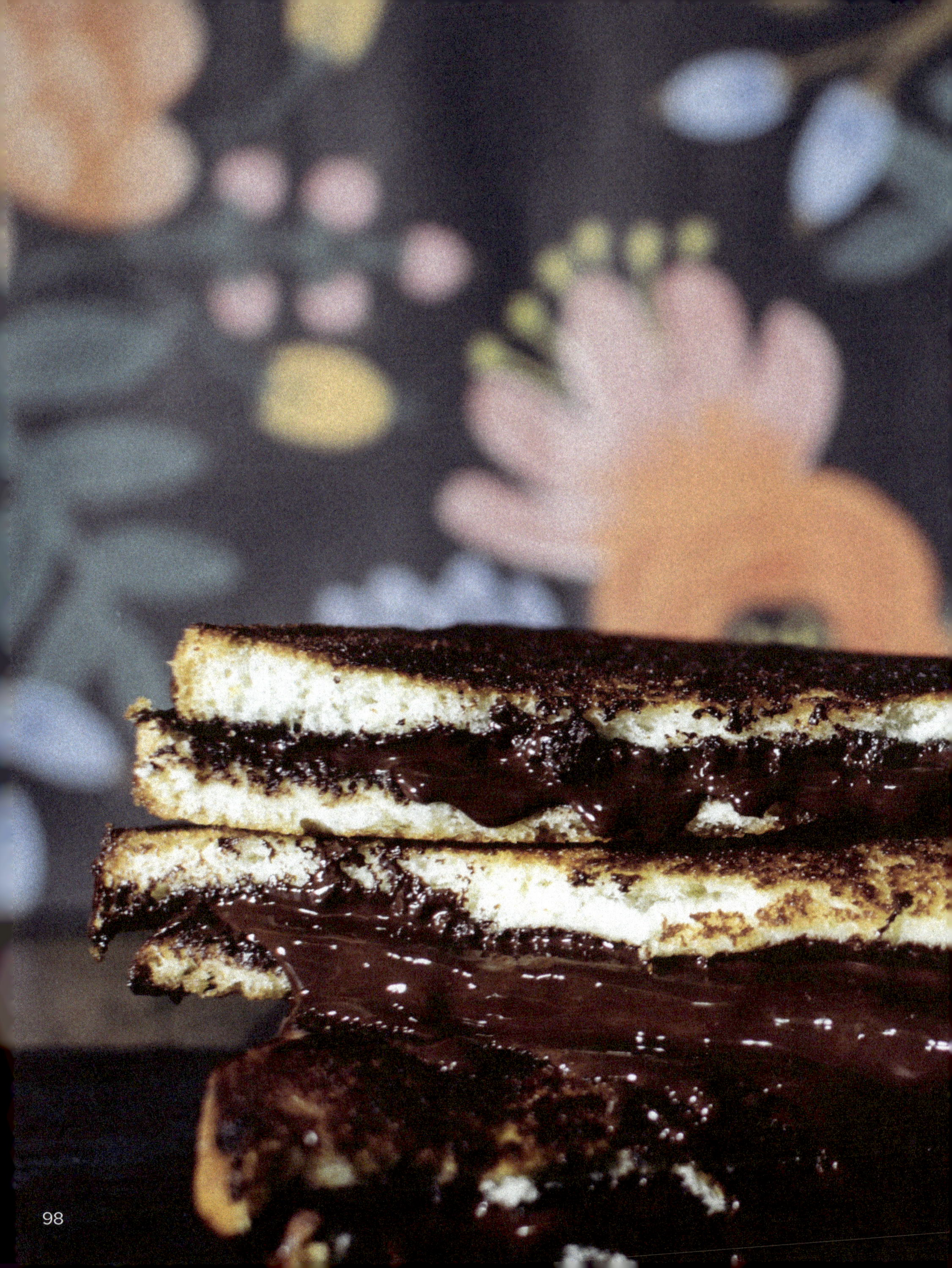

Feeling kinda sad.
Chocolate sandwich

I make this when I'm craving a warm, chocolatey dessert but don't want to be bothered with making brownies or cakes or mixing a bunch of ingredients together and waiting for them to bake. Just let the chocolate cry into your mouth.

MAKES 1 SANDWICH IN ABOUT 10 MINUTES

2 slices of Hawaiian or egg bread

2 oz (about 1/4 cup) chopped chocolate

Maldon salt

butter, room temperature

Pretend like you're making a grilled cheese, but use chocolate instead.

In case you've never made a grilled cheese before:

Heat a skillet over medium high heat.

Butter one side of each slice of bread. Place one slice in the pan over medium heat, butter side down, and top with chopped chocolate and a little sprinkle of sea salt. Top with the other slice of bread, butter side up. Once the chocolate gets melty, flip and brown the other side. Cut on a diagonal, because that's the only way sandwiches taste good.

Notes: I've made this chocolate sandwich with everything from fancy sea salt dark chocolate to a chopped up Snickers bar and let me tell you something: any combination of chocolate, bread and butter will never disappoint.

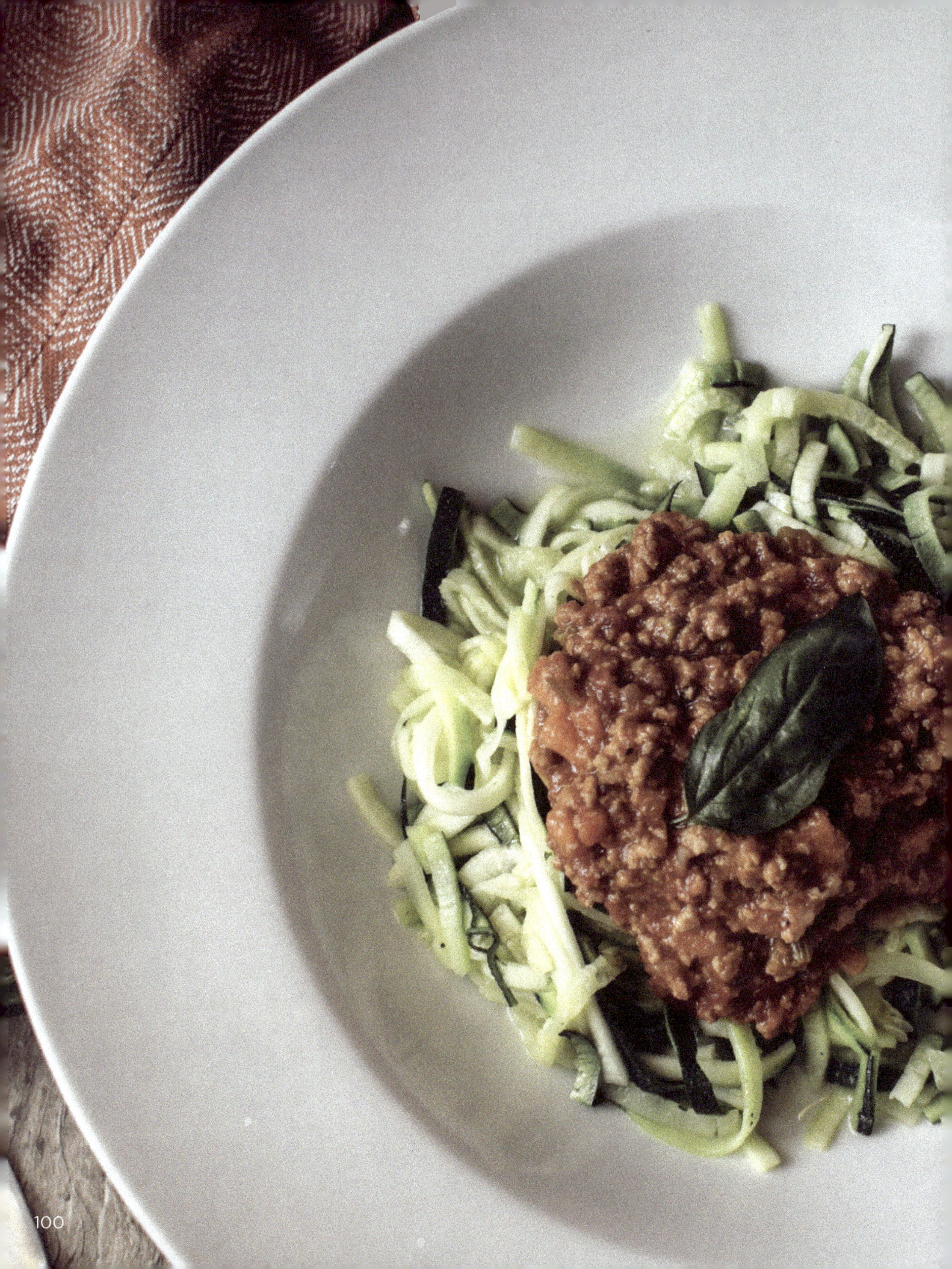

STRESSED

I need to knead something. Or beat something. Or pick at something meaty, like oxtails, instead of like, my emotional scabs.

Turkey bolognese with zucchini noodles (pg. 103)

Oxtail beef patties (pg. 104)

Pretzel buns (pg. 107)

Onion kulcha (pg. 108)

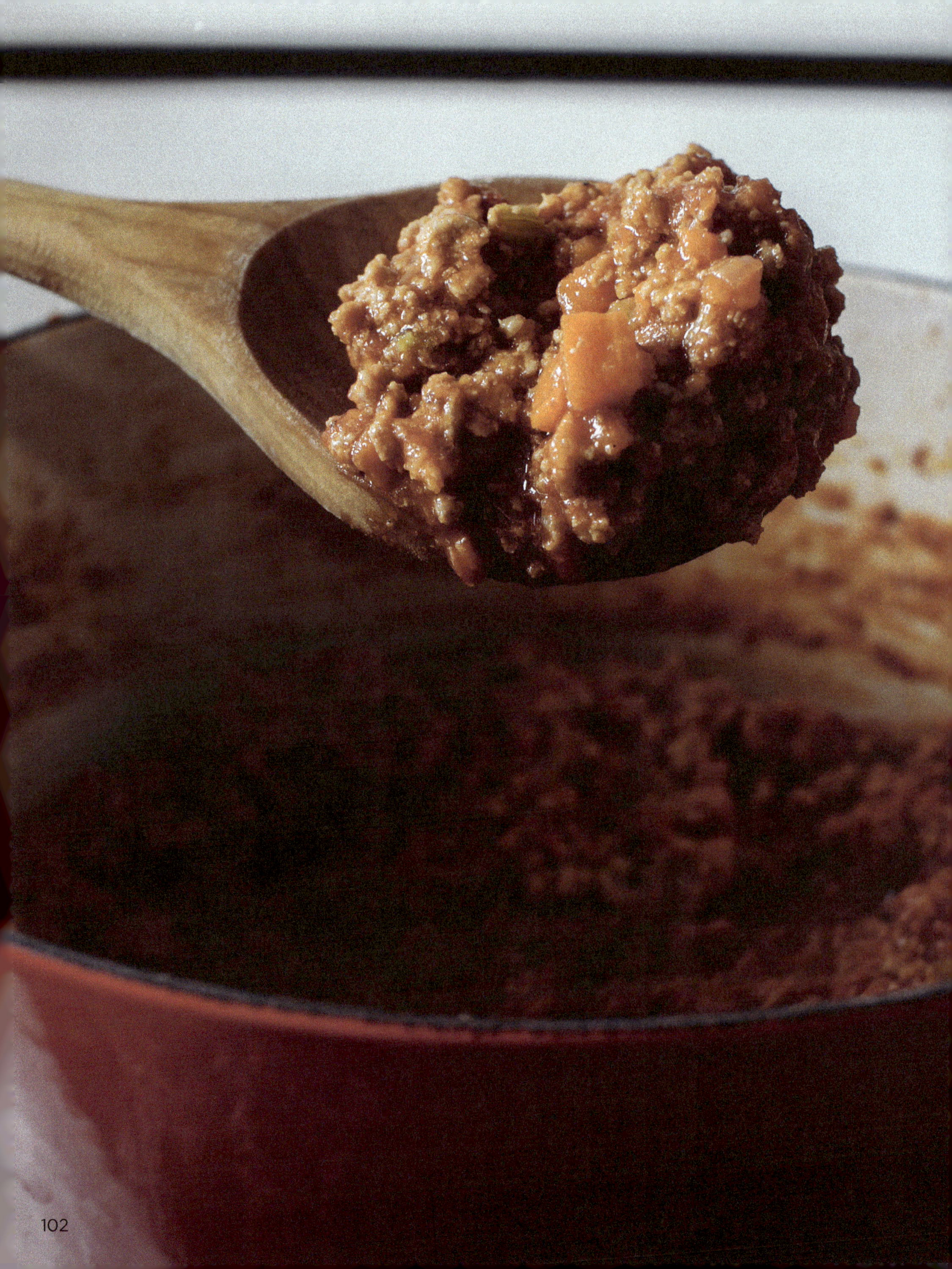

Feeling kinda stressed.

Turkey bolognese with zucchini noodles

This bolognese is inspired by Marcella Hazan's famous recipe, using ground turkey and zucchini noodles instead of pasta for a filling, low-carb meal. I also find there's something very soothing about creating ribbons of noodles out of zucchini.

MAKES 4 SERVINGS IN ABOUT 3 HOURS

vegetable oil

3 tbsp butter

1 small onion, chopped

1 carrot, diced

3 ribs celery, diced

1 lb ground turkey

salt and freshly ground pepper

1 cup whole milk

1 tsp grated nutmeg

1 cup dry white wine

1-28oz can whole San Marzano tomatoes

3 large zucchini, spiralized

1/4 cup grated Parmesan cheese

Sweat the veggies: Place a large pot over medium heat and add in 1 tbsp oil, butter and chopped onions. Cook onions until they're translucent, about 3 minutes. Add in the chopped celery and carrots and stir to coat them in the butter and oil. Cook for another 2 minutes.

Brown the meat: Add in the ground turkey and season with 1/4 tsp of salt and a few grinds of freshly ground pepper. Use a wooden spoon to crumble the turkey and cook until it's no longer pink.

Reduce the liquids: Add in the milk and let simmer gently over low heat, stirring frequently, until it's evaporated completely. Add in a few shavings of nutmeg, about 1/8 teaspoon, and stir to combine. Add in the wine and, once again, let simmer until it's mostly evaporated.

Simmer the sauce: Add in the tomatoes and stir to combine. Once the sauce begins to bubble, turn the heat down to low to maintain a gentle, lazy simmer. Continue to cook, uncovered, for 3 hours or more, stirring occasionally. If you find the sauce begins to dry out and stick during cooking, add about 1/2 cup of water as necessary. The sauce is done when there's no more water and you can see the fat separate from the rest of the sauce. Taste and season with additional salt and pepper as needed.

Saute the zucchini noodles: Heat 1 tbsp oil in a large skillet over medium-high heat. Add in zucchini noodles and cook until tender but still crisp, about 1-2 minutes.

Serve sauce over zucchini and garnish with Parmesan cheese.

Feeling kinda stressed.

Oxtail beef patties

I love eating oxtail, but I EXTRALY love it when I can eat it without having to pick through any bones. De-boned oxtail meat is such a luxury to me because all the time and love that goes into removing small bits of meat from tiny bones. This is probably my favorite recipe in the book.

MAKES 10-12 PATTIES IN ABOUT 1 HOUR 30 MINUTES

for the dough

- 4 cups all-purpose flour
- 2 tsp salt
- 2 tsp turmeric
- 1 tsp curry powder
- 1 1/2 cups cold butter-flavored shortening, cubed

for the oxtails

- 3 lbs oxtails
- salt and pepper
- 1 tbsp vegetable oil
- 1 bunch green onion, chopped
- 1 large onion, chopped
- 3 cloves garlic, crushed
- 1 bay leaf
- 2 sprigs fresh thyme
- 10 allspice berries
- 2" ginger, peeled and sliced
- 3 tbsp soy sauce
- 1 tbsp Worcestershire
- 2-3 cups beef broth, enough to almost cover.

Make the dough: In a large bowl, combine flour, salt, turmeric and curry powder. Add in the shortening and use your fingers to work it into the flour. When the shortening is in pea-sized pieces, add in 1/2 cup of ice water and gently mix with your finger tips. Add additional ice water as needed, a spoonful or two at a time, until the dough begins to come together. Knead the dough for a couple minutes; the dough should feel a bit more smooth. Form dough into a disc and cover in plastic wrap. Let the dough chill while the oxtails are cooking.

Make the oxtails: Season the oxtails generously with salt and pepper. In a pressure cooker on high heat, add vegetable oil and brown the oxtails on all sides. Add in the onion, garlic, bay leaf, thyme, allspice, ginger, green onions, soy sauce Worcestershire and beef broth and attach pressure cooker lid. Once it comes to pressure, cook for 45 minutes. Let pressure release naturally. Alternately, if you don't have a pressure cooker, braise oxtails in a dutch oven until tender, about 2 1/2 - 3 hours.

Pick the meat: Remove oxtails from the pot. Strain the solids and discard them, reserving 1/4 cup of the cooking liquid. Pick the meat from the cooled oxtails and discard the bones. Mix the oxtail meat with a couple spoonfuls of the reserved cooking liquid, use more as needed to keep meat moist. Taste, and adjust seasonings as you like.

Roll the dough: Heat oven to 375F. Remove the dough from the refrigerator and divide into 4 pieces. Lightly flour your rolling surface. Beginning with one piece, roll out to about 12"x12", large enough to cut out three or four 6" circles (use a soup bowl to cut circles). Repeat with the rest of the dough re-rolling leftover scraps to make more patties.

Make the patties: Place about 2 tbsp of oxtail on one side of the dough circle. Dip your finger in a bit of water and wet the edges of the dough. Gently fold the dough over the filling and use a fork to crimp the edges together. Repeat until you're out of dough or out of filling. Place patties on a non-stick baking sheet and bake until golden brown, about 25-30 minutes.

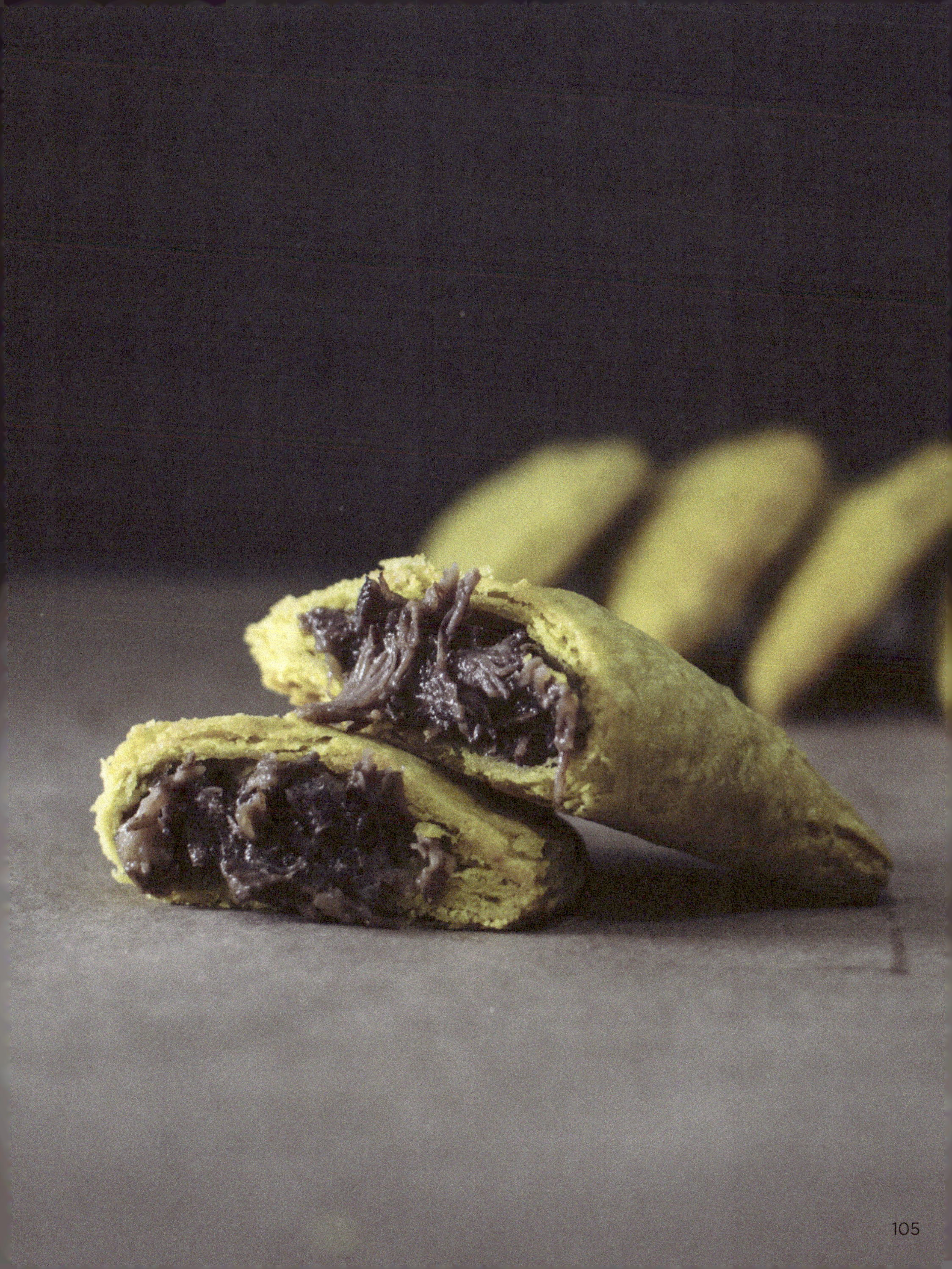

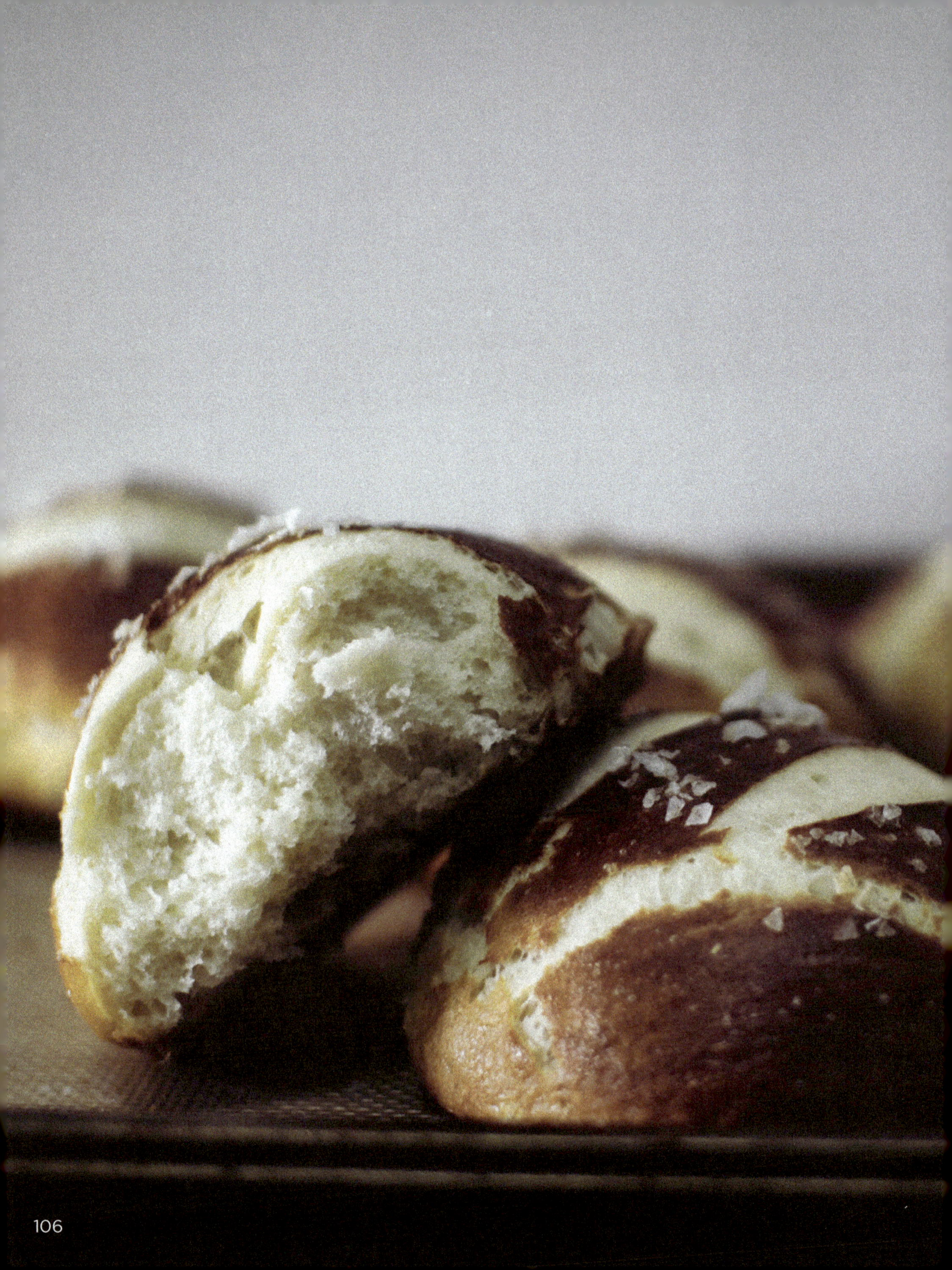

Feeling kinda stressed.

Pretzel buns

Kneading dough is such a great stress reliever. It's like being a little kid again and playing with Play-Doh, except you get to bake it and eat it after. These are also the base for the pretzel bread pudding on page 24.

MAKES 12 BUNS IN ABOUT 2 HOURS

---

1 1/2 cups warm water (110°F)

1 package (2 1/4 tsp) active dry yeast

2 teaspoons sugar

4 1/2 cups unbleached all-purpose flour

2 teaspoons sea salt

4 tablespoons unsalted butter, melted

1/4 cup baking soda

1 whole egg, lightly beaten

coarse sea salt or pretzel salt

Bloom the yeast: In a large bowl, add warm water, yeast and sugar. Stir to combine and let rest for 5-10 minutes, until yeast blooms. It'll look foamy and you'll see bubbles popping up.

Proof the dough: Add the flour, salt, and melted butter to the bowl with the yeast. Using a wooden spoon, mix until well combined. Turn dough out onto a lightly floured surface and knead until smooth and elastic, about 10 minutes. Place in an oiled bowl and cover with plastic wrap or a clean, lint-free towel and let rise in a warm place for 1 hour, or until doubled.

Form the buns: Line a large baking sheet with parchment paper and set aside. Punch down the dough and turn onto a lightly floured surface. Divide the dough into 8 equal pieces (about 4.5-5 oz each). To shape the dough into rolls, start forming the round shape by pulling the edges of the dough toward the center, pinching them together to form a seam. Place dough ball on the prepared baking sheet and repeat with remaining dough. Once all dough has been formed, cover the baking sheet with towel and let dough rise in a warm place for 30 minutes.

Poach the pretzels: Once the second rise has finished, preheat oven to 425F. In a large pot, combine 2 quarts of water and 1/4 cup of baking soda and bring to a rolling boil. This is the pretzel poaching liquid that gives that shiny, brown, chewy crust.

Place 2-3 of the rolls at a time into the baking soda solution, seam side down. Poach for 30 seconds, then carefully turn the roll over and poach for another 30 seconds. Remove with a slotted spoon to the same prepared sheet pan, seam side down. Repeat with the remaining dough.

Bake the buns: Brush each roll with the beaten egg, making sure to brush the sides as well. Sprinkle with kosher or pretzel salt. Using a sharp, straight-edged knife, cut 2 slashes or an "X" in each roll, cutting about 1/4" deep. Bake the rolls in the preheated oven for 15-20 minutes, until golden brown.

Feeling kinda stressed.

Onion kulcha with cucumber lime yogurt

Kulcha is like naan's less fussy, non-yeast based cousin. It's a great little stuffed flat bread that works as a starter or a side. Get creative with the fillings, use what you have on hand and make the recipe your own. Do it for the kulcha.

MAKES 10 KULCHA IN ABOUT 1 HOUR

---

for the cucumber yogurt
- 3 small cucumbers, grated (about 1 1/2 cups)
- 1/4 tsp kosher salt
- 1 1/2 cups Greek yogurt
- 1 lime, zest and juice
- 1 clove garlic, minced
- 1 tbsp chopped mint leaves
- 2 tbsp butter, browned (optional)

for the dough
- 3 cups all-purpose flour
- 1/2 tsp baking powder
- 1/8 tsp baking soda
- 1 tbsp sugar
- 1 tsp kosher salt
- 1/4 cup vegetable oil
- 1/2 cup Greek yogurt
- 1 tbsp ghee, plus more for cooking

for the filling
- 1 medium onion, finely chopped
- 3 tbsp chopped mint leaves
- 2-3 chilies, finely chopped
- 1/2 tsp dried oregano
- 1/4 tsp kosher salt
- 1 tbsp finely chopped fresh ginger

Make the sauce: Place the grated cucumber in a colander, and sprinkle 1/4 kosher salt over. Massage the salt into the cucumber and let drain for 20 minutes. Squeeze out as much of the water as you can.

In a small saucepan, cook the butter over medium heat until it smells nutty and takes on a brown color, about 5 minutes.

In a medium bowl, combine the yogurt, zest and juice of one lime, garlic and most of the mint leaves and most of the butter, reserving some of each for garnish. Top with remaining mint and drizzle the remaining butter over the top.

Make the dough: In a medium bowl, add the flour, baking powder, baking soda, sugar and salt. Stir to combine. Add in the vegetable oil, yogurt, ghee. Stir to mix, adding in water until a soft dough forms. I added about 1 cup of water. The dough will look a bit rough and be quite sticky. Turn the dough out onto a lightly floured surface and knead until smooth and elastic, about 5 minutes. Place in an oiled bowl, turning the dough in the bowl to coat with oil, and cover. Let rest for one hour.

Make the filling: Combine the chopped onion, chopped mint leaves, finely chopped chilies, oregano, salt and ginger.

Fill the dough: Once the dough has rested, divide into 10 equal pieces and shape into balls. Let rest an additional 10 minutes. Lightly sprinkle flour on both sides of dough ball and roll out into a circle, about 6" in diameter. Sprinkle about 2 tbsp of the filling on one half of the dough round, fold the other half over and press firmly along the edges to seal. Use a rolling pin to roll filled dough to seal completely.

Cook the kulcha: In a cast-iron skillet (or any other large, heavy bottomed pan), place a bit of ghee or vegetable oil. Cook the kulcha over medium-high heat until bubbles begin to appear on the surface and the bottom has browned nicely. Flip and continue to cook until browned - about 5 minutes per side. Brush the top of the cooked kulcha with a bit of ghee or butter.

109

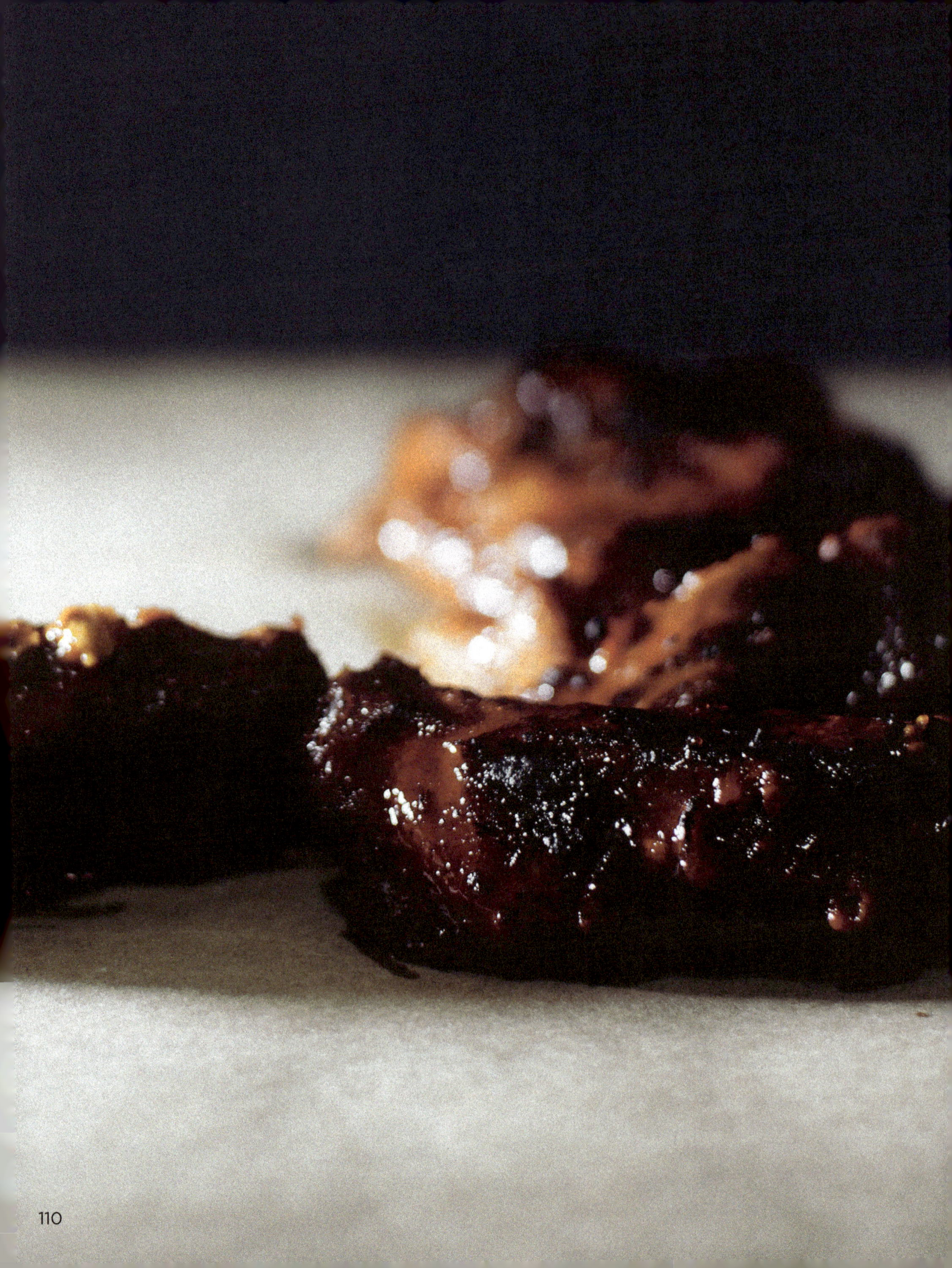

THANKFUL

Sharing is caring, and what better way to show your appreciation for the people you love than to feed them delicious foods? These recipes can be scaled easily to feed a crowd, are relatively inexpensive to make and great for sharing with my people. If you only make one thing out of this chapter (out of this book, really), please let it be the Spicy red ribs, because OMG PLS.

Salt and pepper chicken thighs (pg. 113)

Japchae (pg. 114)

Spicy red ribs (pg. 116)

Sticky wings (pg. 118)

Pancit (pg. 121)

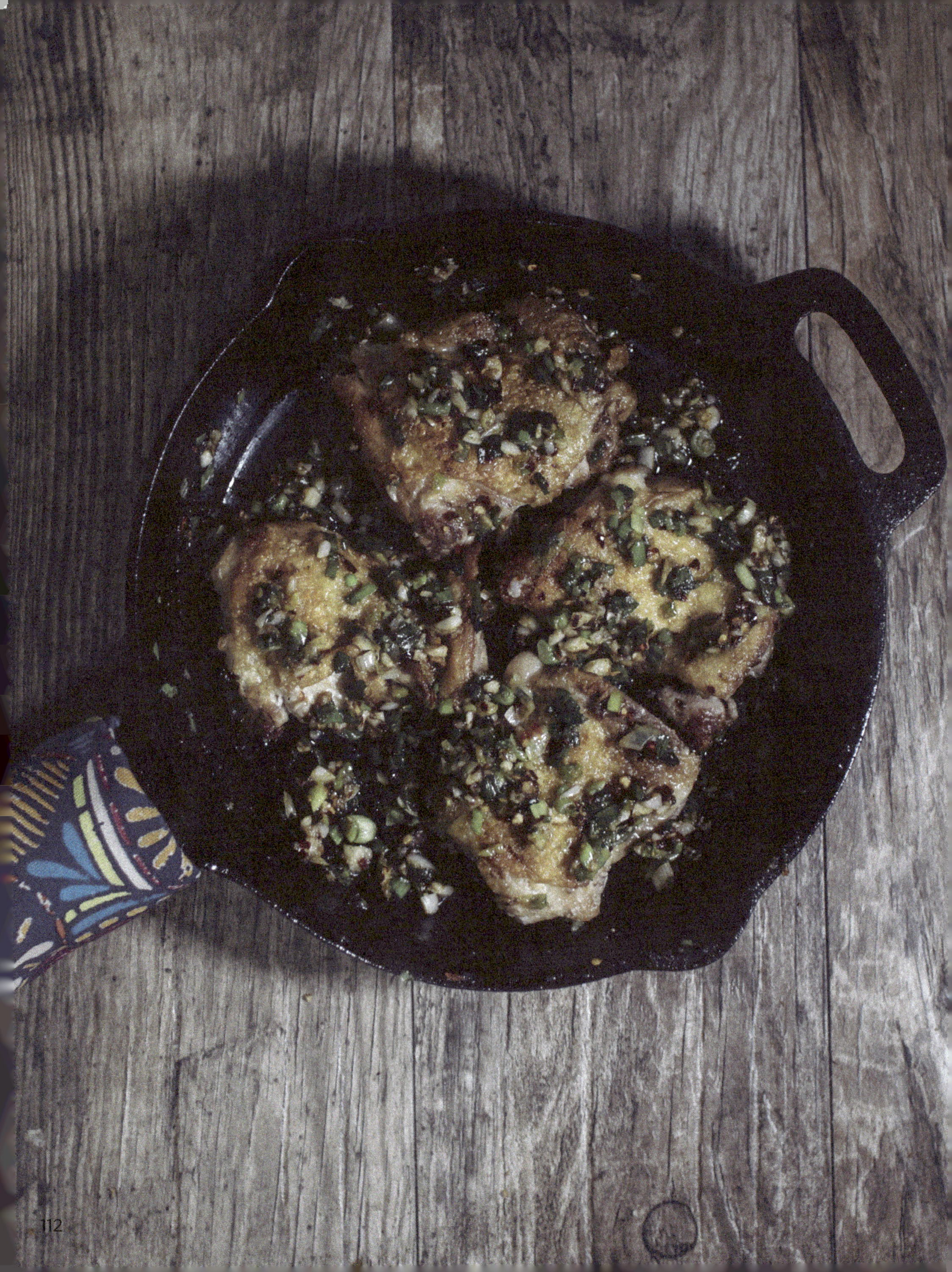

Feeling kinda thankful.

Salt and pepper chicken thighs

A play on salt and pepper chicken wings, this version gives the same flavor and crunchy skin, without all of the oil and deep frying.

MAKES 4 SERVINGS IN ABOUT 30 MINUTES

- 4-6 chicken thighs; skin-on, bones removed
- kosher salt
- white pepper (major key - don't substitute this)
- 1 head garlic, finely chopped
- 1 bunch green onion, finely chopped
- 1-2 tbsp chili flakes, to taste

Brown the chicken skin: Dry chicken with paper towel. Remove the bone with kitchen shears and trim any excess fat. Salt skin generously. Season meat side with about 1 tsp salt and 1 tsp white pepper. Heat a large pan over medium-high (cast iron is great for this). Put the chicken in the pan, skin-side down, then leave it alone - the fat needs to render for the skin to crisp up. Let skin side fry until crispy and golden brown, about 10-12 minutes; use a splatter guard to keep the oil from going all over the place. Flip chicken, cook an additional 3-5 minutes or more, until cooked through. Let drain on paper towels.

Season it up: While the chicken rests, remove all but about 2 tbsp chicken fat from the pan and add garlic; saute over medium heat until fragrant, about 1 minute. Add in the chili flakes and green onions and cook a couple more minutes. Season with 1 tsp white pepper and 1 tsp salt; taste and adjust seasonings as needed. Pour over crispy chicken thighs.

Feeling kinda thankful.

Japchae

My friends LOVE this recipe. It's also great for meal prepping and using up any veggies in the fridge that are about to go bad. This recipe is pretty versatile - make it yours! I know this looks like a lot of ingredients, but it's pretty much the same few things over and over again.

MAKES 6 IN ABOUT 1 HOUR 15 MINUTES

---

for the beef
- 1 lb boneless ribeye, cut into thin strips
- 2 tsp sesame oil
- 2 tbsp gochujang
- 1 tsp rice wine vinegar
- 1 tbsp garlic, minced
- 1 tbsp ginger, grated
- 1 tbsp soy sauce
- 1 tbsp vegetable oil
- salt and pepper

for the noodle and mushroom sauce
- 6 tbsp soy sauce
- 1 tbsp honey
- 1 tbsp sesame oil
- 3.5 oz shiitake mushrooms, sliced

for the spinach
- 10 oz baby spinach
- 1 tbsp vegetable oil
- 2 tsp garlic
- 1 tsp sesame oil

for the veggies
- sesame oil
- kosher salt
- 1/2 large red bell pepper, julienned
- 1/2 cup sliced onion
- 1/2 cup julienned carrots

for the noodles
- 12 oz sweet potato noodles
- 2 tbsp soy sauce

Marinate the beef: Combine the sliced beef, sesame oil, gochujang, rice wine vinegar, garlic, ginger and soy sauce in a bowl and let marinate for 1 hour.

Make the sauce: In a small bowl, combine soy sauce, honey and sesame oil. Pour half of the sauce over the mushrooms, and reserve the other half for the noodles.

Cook the spinach: In a large skillet, heat 1 tbsp vegetable oil over medium high heat. Saute spinach until just wilted. Let drain in a strainer until cool, squeezing out extra water. Season spinach with garlic, sesame oil and salt.

Cook the vegetables: Wipe out the pan. Cook bell pepper, onion and carrots individually until tender crisp, about 1-2 minutes each, using a drizzle of sesame oil and a pinch of salt for each time you saute. Place the vegetables in a large bowl. Wipe out the pan and saute the marinated mushrooms for about 3-4 minutes; add to the bowl of vegetables.

Cook the beef: Wipe out the skillet and add 1 tbsp of vegetable oil. Cook the beef over high heat, about 4-5 minutes, until no longer pink. Add to the bowl of vegetables.

Cook the noodles: Bring a pot of water to a boil and season with 2 tbsp of soy sauce. Cook sweet potato noodles for 6-8 minutes, until cooked through. Drain noodles and rinse with cold water. Use kitchen shears to make a few cuts through the noodles so they're a bit shorter, if you like. Add noodles to the bowl with the vegetables and meat and add in the remaining sauce. Toss to combine.

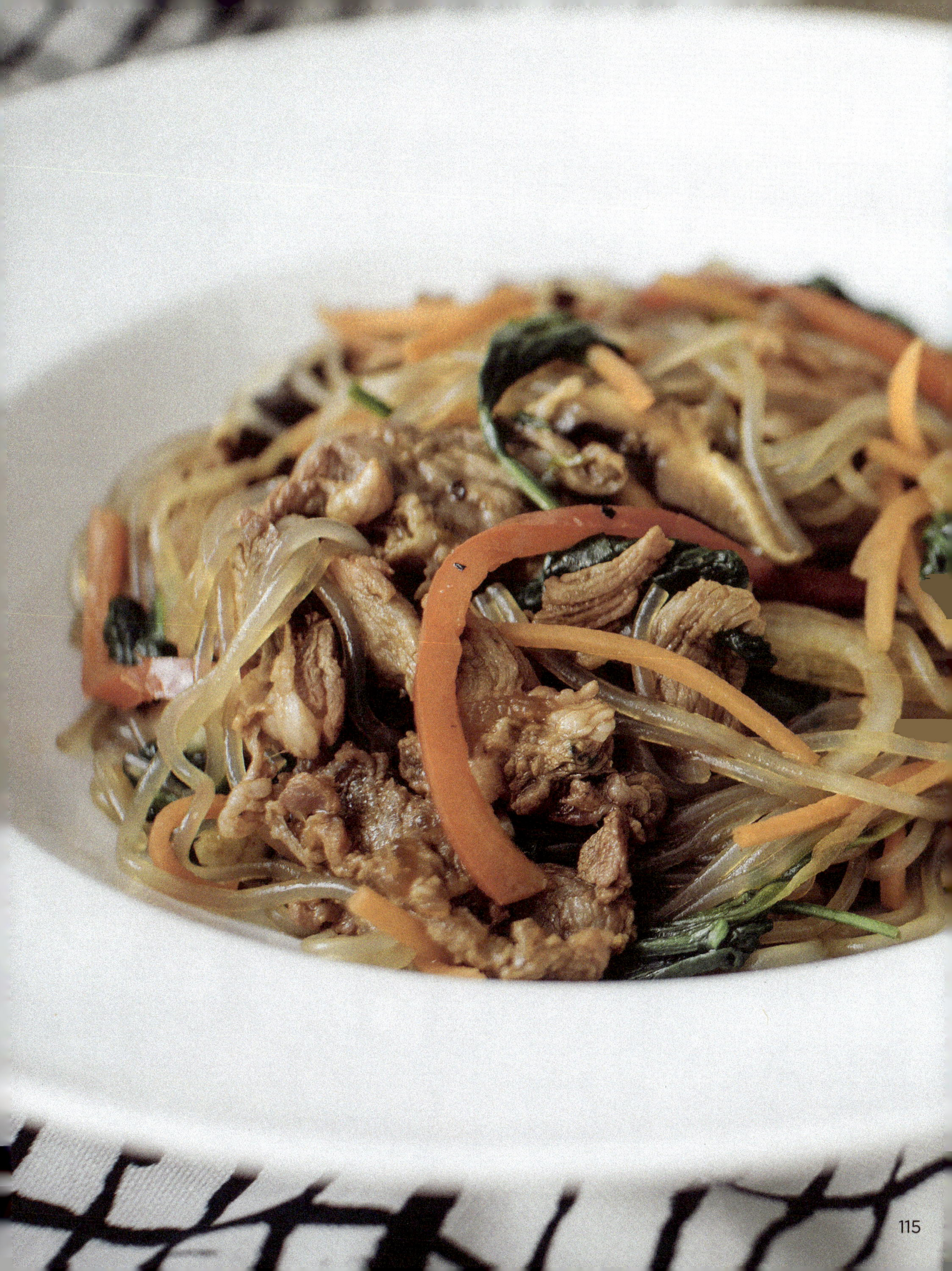

Feeling kinda thankful,
Spicy red ribs

I Columbus'd this recipe from my best friend Jonathan's Aunt Tracie's long-time friend Jean. Thanks Auntie Jean! This recipe is a game changer, and the sauce used to marinate the ribs also works well with chicken wings or pork loin or as a dip for chicken nuggets, if that's your thing. I'm begging you to make these.

MAKES 6 SERVINGS IN ABOUT 3 HOURS

---

2 cups gochujang (Korean hot pepper paste)

2 cups sugar

6 cloves garlic, chopped

2" ginger, peeled and chopped

1 cup sake

2 tbsp sesame oil

1 bunch green onions, chopped

4-5 lbs baby back ribs

Make the sauce: Preheat oven to 275F. Combine gochujang, sugar, garlic, ginger, sake and green onions in a large bowl. Taste it - the sauce should be sweet and spicy and the consistency of spaghetti sauce. Adjust any seasonings and set aside 1/2 cup of sauce.

Cook the ribs: Using kitchen shears or a sharp knife, cut ribs into individual bones. Toss ribs in the bowl with the sauce. Line a baking dish with a couple layers of foil and place ribs side by side. Cover tightly with more foil and cook for 2 - 2 1/2 hours, until tender.

Char the ribs: Remove the foil from the pan and brush the ribs with reserved sauce. Set oven to broil and cook ribs another 4-5 minutes, until slightly charred in spots. Alternately, grill the ribs until burnty and delicious.

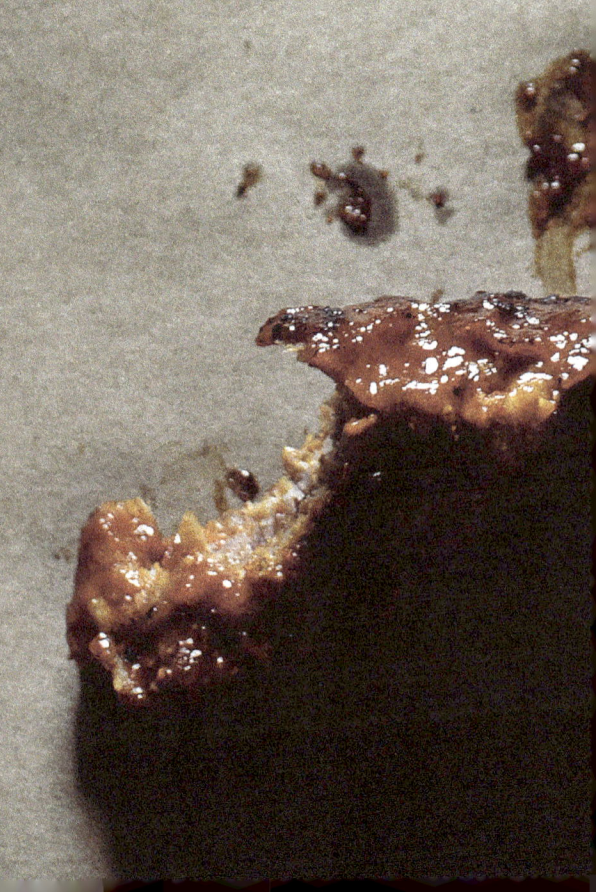

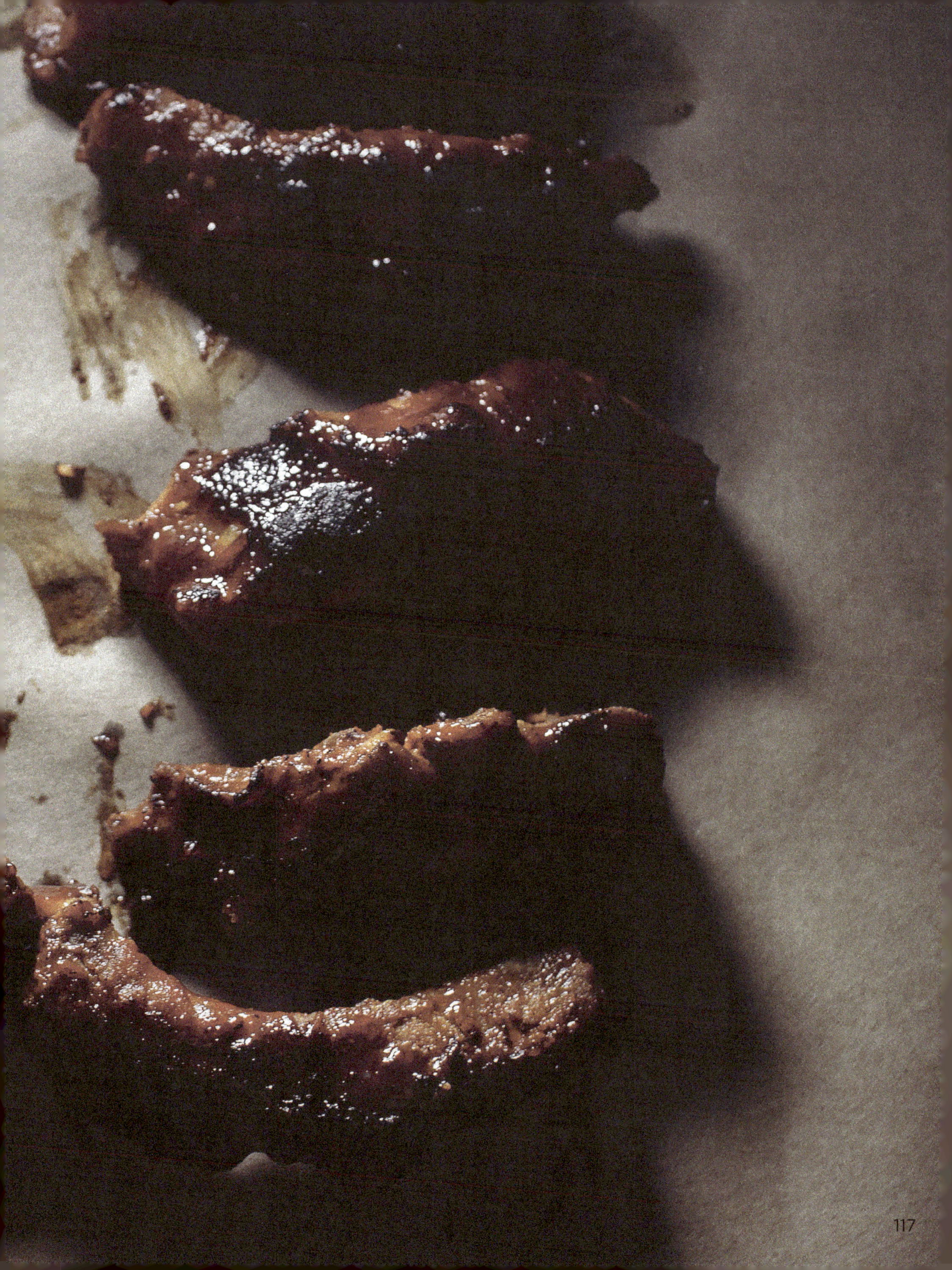

Feeling kinda thankful.

Sticky wings

It's a one-pot crowd pleaser. Not all wings have to be fried, sometimes they're just as good sticky.

MAKES 4 SERVINGS IN ABOUT 45 MINUTES

- 3 lbs chicken wings, split
- 2 tbsp chopped fresh ginger
- 2 Thai bird chiles, finely chopped
- 1/3 cup soy sauce
- 1/3 cup sake
- 2 tsp Chinese five spice powder
- 3 tbsp hoisin sauce
- 3 tbsp rice wine vinegar
- 3 tbsp brown sugar
- 2 green onions, thinly sliced
- limes, for serving

Brown the chicken: In a large skillet with a lid, cook the wings over medium heat, turning once, until browned on both sides, about 6-7 minutes each side. Work in batches if necessary.

Make it sticky: Add the ginger and chopped chiles to the chicken and saute for about a minute. Add in soy sauce, sake, five spice, hoisin sauce, rice wine vinegar, brown sugar and 1/4 cup of water. Bring to a simmer over medium heat, then cover the pan and cook for 10 minutes. Uncover, and turn up the heat to medium-high. Stir the wings occasionally until cooked through and the sauce has thickened, about 10 more minutes.

Serve with lime wedges and garnish with green onions.

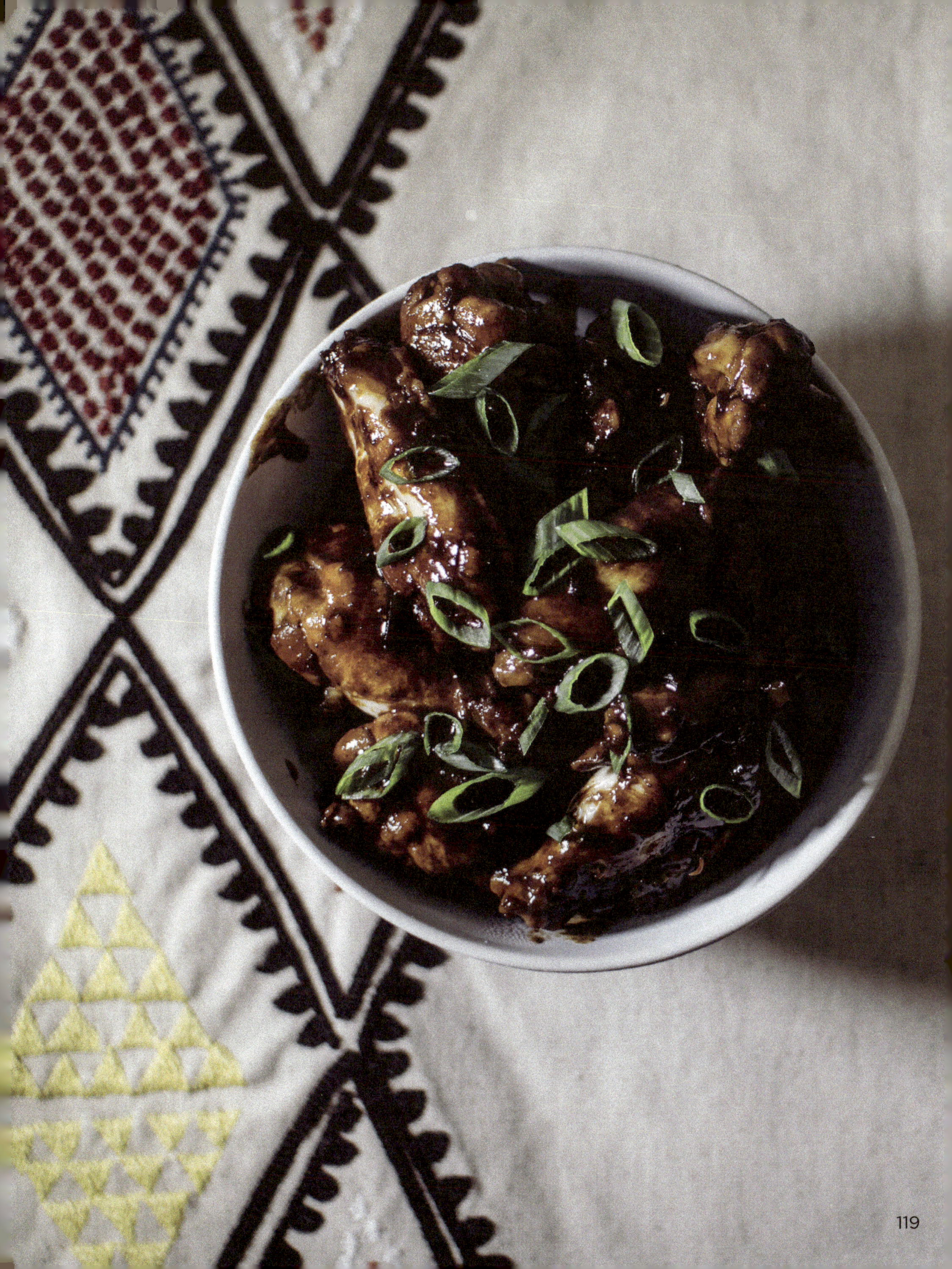

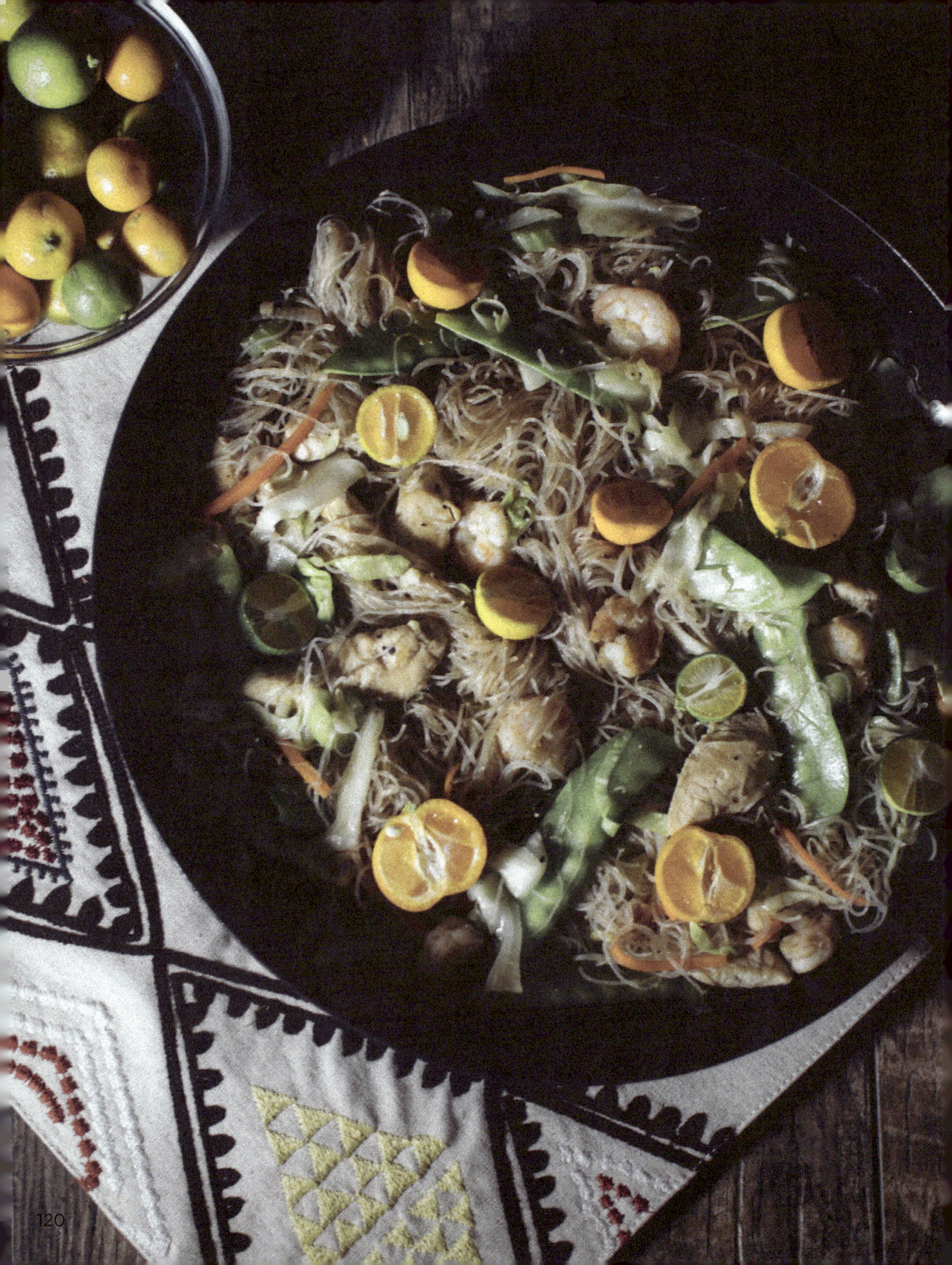

Feeling kinda thankful.
Pancit

Pancit is in the same realm as "rice", as far as Filipino food staples. If you go to a Filipino party and there isn't a flimsy metal tray of pancit, something's wrong or someone's late.

MAKES 8 SERVINGS IN ABOUT 45 MINUTES

---

16 oz pancit noodles (rice noodle sticks)

vegetable oil

1/2 lb chicken thighs, thinly sliced

1/2 lb shrimp, peeled and deveined

3 cloves garlic, chopped

1 onion, chopped

3 1/2 cups of chicken broth

1 cup snow peas

1 cup shredded carrots

2 cups chopped cabbage

1 cup sliced celery

1/4 cup soy sauce, more to taste

calamansi or lemon, for serving

Soak the noodles: Soak rice noodles in hot water for 5 minutes, then drain. Do not oversoak the noodles or they'll break down.

Cook the meats: In a wok or large pot, add a drizzle a bit of oil and add in the shrimp. Season with salt and pepper and cook until just done, about 1-2 minutes. Set aside in a large bowl. Add a bit more oil to the wok, then add the chicken and season with salt and pepper. Once cooked through, remove and set aside with the shrimp.

Cook the veggies: Add a bit of oil to the wok and saute garlic and onion. Add in broth, snow peas, carrots, cabbage and celery. Let cook for a few minutes, until the cabbage softens a bit. Remove the veggies with a slotted spoon and set them aside with the shrimp and chicken, leaving the liquid in the wok.

Cook the noodles: Add the soy sauce to the wok. Add in the soaked noodles and mix well. Cook the noodles until the liquid evaporates. Add the vegetables, chicken and shrimp back to the wok and toss to combine. Taste, adding more soy sauce to if needed. Serve with calamansi or lemon slices.

RECIPE INDEX

BREADS
28 Honey pandesal
82 Gorgonzola and bacon drop biscuits
107 Pretzel buns
108 Onion kulcha

BEEF
18 Lumpia
47 Korean BBQ tostadas
74 Corned beef and rice
91 Sesame beef and spinach bowl
104 Oxtail beef patties
114 Japchae

CHICKEN
37 Smoked honey wings
38 Smoked chicken and dumplings
48 Vietnamese fried chicken bun
57 Chicken shawarma with tabbouleh
69 Arroz caldo
70 Chicken kare-kare
92 Chicken adobo
113 Salt and pepper chicken thighs
118 Sticky wings

NOODLES & DUMPLINGS
14 Pancit molo
17 Lamb dumplings in chili sauce
114 Japchae
121 Pancit

PORK
18 Lumpia
43 Jerk pork belly bao
73 Eggplant omelette (Tortang talong)
77 Pork belly sisig
116 Spicy red ribs

SAUCES AND DIPS
04 Toum
07 Corn salsa
07 Baba ganoush
09 Smoked almond gremolata

SEAFOOD
44 Po Mì
54 A good tuna salad
62 Salmon with gremolata and baby broccoli
86 Shrimp and mascarpone grits
96 BBQ shrimp toast

SWEETS & DESSERTS
24 Pretzel bread pudding with brown sugar bourbon
27 Brown butter caramel rice krispie treats
65 $20,000 chocolate cake
99 Chocolate sandwich

TURKEY
33 Chipotle turkey chili
34 White beans with smoked turkey
85 A carton soup and meatballs
103 Turkey bolognese with zucchini noodles

VEGETARIAN
13 Mushroom and quinoa potstickers
23 Marsala mushroom lasagna
53 Brown butter chili eggs
58 Peanut and lime sugar snap peas
61 Roasted brussels sprouts with garlic tahini
81 Labneh toasts
95 Spinach soup